CAPTAIN'S LOG

Three years since the traumatic events of *Star Trek Into Darkness*, the cinematic adventures of the *Enterprise* crew continue, in the critically-acclaimed movie, *Star Trek Beyond*.

In this *Star Trek Beyond* movie special, we tell the full story of the making of the new *Star Trek* installment, from inception to world premiere, and take you even further behind-the-scenes with in-depth new features and an array of previously unpublished photos.

Discover what has changed for the *Enterprise* crew, half-way through their five-year mission, in exclusive interviews with stars Chris Pine (Kirk), Zachary Quinto (Spock), Zoe Saldana (Uhura), Karl Urban (McCoy), John Cho (Sulu), Simon Pegg (Scotty), and the much-missed Anton Yelchin (Chekov).

Guest stars Sofia Boutella (the unforgettable Jaylah) and Shohreh Aghdashloo (Commodore Paris) talk about the joys of joining the *Trek* family, while Simon Pegg and Doug Jung reveal the challenges they faced in writing a *Star Trek* adventure for the big screen, in the shadow of the show's fiftieth anniversary. We explore the movie's VFX, stunning make-up, and incredible costumes, and Justin Lin discusses his approach to directing *Beyond*, plus we take a long, hard look at the movie's terrifying villain, Krall (Idris Elba).

It's an incredible journey.

Christopher Cooper
Editor

In Memory of
Anton Yelchin,
1989 – 2016

EDITORIAL

- **Editor:** Christopher Cooper
- **Senior Editor:** Martin Eden
- **Designer:** Dan Bura
- **Contributors:** Bryan Cairns, Chris Dows, Rich Matthews, Ian Spelling, and K.Stoddard Hayes.
- **Bad Robot:** J.J. Abrams, Bryan Burk, Damon Lindelof, David Baronoff
- **CBS Consumer Products:** John Van Citters and Marian Cordry
- **Copyright Promotions Ltd.:** Anna Hatjoullis
- **Paramount Home Entertainment:** Kate Addy, Jiella Esmat, Liz Hadley and John Robson
- **Simon & Schuster US:** Ed Schlesinger
- **SPECIAL THANKS** Michelle Alt and Diana Pearson at Paramount Pictures; Omaze; Justin Lin, Simon Pegg, Doug Jung and the entire cast and crew of Star Trek Beyond.

TITAN

- **Editorial Assistant:** Tolly Maggs
- **Production Supervisors:** Maria Pearson & Jackie Flook
- **Production Assistant** Peter James
- **Production Manager** Obi Onoura
- **Art Director:** Oz Browne
- **Senior Sales Manager:** Steve Tothill
- **Direct Sales & Marketing Manager:** Ricky Claydon
- **US Advertising Manager:** Jeni Smith
- **Brand Manager:** Lucy Ripper
- **Advertising Assistant:** Jessica Reid
- **Circulation Assistant:** Daniel Downes
- **Commercial Manager:** Michelle Fairlamb
- **Publishing Manager:** Darryl Tothill
- **Publishing Director:** Chris Teather
- **Operations Director:** Leigh Baulch
- **Executive Director:** Vivian Cheung
- **Publisher:** Nick Landau

STAR TREK

STAR TREK BEYOND COLLECTORS EDITION
Published by Titan Magazines, 144 Southwark Street, London SE1 0UP. TM ® & © 2016 CBS Studios Inc. © 2016 Paramount Pictures. STAR TREK and Related Marks and Logos are Trademarks of CBS Studios Inc. All Rights Reserved. Titan Authorised User. CBS, the CBS Eye logo and related marks are trademarks of CBS Broadcasting Inc. TM & © 2016 CBS Broadcasting Inc. All rights reserved. For sale in the US, UK, Eire, Australia and New Zealand.
Printed in the US.
ISBN: 9781785860096

First Edition November 2016.
10 9 8 7 6 5 4 3 2 1
US NEWSSTAND DISTRIBUTION:
Total Publishers Services Inc,
John Dziewiatkowski,
610-851-7683

CONTENTS

STAR TREK BEYOND
COLLECTORS EDITION

MAKING BEYOND

FEATURES

WARP SPEED

Star Trek has been a lifelong love for indie-turned-blockbuster director Justin Lin. Widely known for his work on the hugely successful *Fast & Furious* movies, it was Lin's independent films that first won him acclaim amongst cinemagoers and critics alike. It was that unique combination of an artistic eye and a flair for action that earned him a seat in the captain's chair for *Star Trek Beyond*...

Words: Bryan Cairns

Krall causing havoc

Star Trek Magazine: What does the *Star Trek* franchise mean to you, and what was your entry point into it?

Justin Lin: I was eight years old when my family immigrated to the States from Taiwan. My parents owned a little fish and chips restaurant that closed at 9pm. We had dinner at 10, and *Star Trek* came on at 11. My brothers and I would weasel our way into hanging out with my parents and watch it. From eight to 18, that was my connection. It was the original cast, and my first understanding of what reruns were was through *Star Trek*. As a kid, I thought every day was a new show until they ran out. I remember watching the one with Pike ('The Menagerie'). It didn't make any sense. I was like, "Where's Kirk?" But, looking back now, it had a big impact on me.

I remember as a little kid, we moved halfway around the world. I didn't know how to speak the language. All our cousins and uncles and aunts were half a world away. It was just me, my parents and siblings. The idea of family on *Star Trek* – through shared experience, and it didn't just have to be blood – that really became a part of me. Now I have a six-year-old, and he has Uncle Vin (Diesel). That's my family now. A lot of that came from my experience with *Trek*.

Kirk gets set

The *Enterprise* is attacked

Lin on set with Zachery Quinto

STM: From your perspective, what makes a good *Star Trek* story? What were some of the elements or themes you wanted *Star Trek Beyond* to focus in on?

JL: It's kind of a complex question. *Star Trek* is the one franchise that is able to thrive on different mediums. *Star Trek* should be equally powerful, whether it's two people in a room, or it's a battle in

"*STAR TREK* SHOULD BE EQUALLY POWERFUL, WHETHER IT'S TWO PEOPLE IN A ROOM, OR IT'S A BATTLE IN SPACE."

space. Growing up with it – with the characters, that ensemble – was a big part of *Trek* to me.

At the same time, the mission statement of *Star Trek* is to always be pushing and always be exploring, because you never know what's going to happen the next night, or the next night after. That's the spirit of *Star Trek*. The further you push out, the more it examines who we are. Those are the general ideas of *Trek*. Obviously, we aren't making a TV show, we're making a big-budget movie, but I wanted to make sure we were able to capture and embrace all those elements.

STM: *Star Trek Beyond* takes place two-and-a-half years after *Star Trek Into Darkness*. What were some of the developments that a time jump allowed you to explore?

JL: The irony, a lot of times with franchises, is that you earn your sequel. Usually, in doing that, the hero has a pretty amazing journey. So, especially coming after *Into Darkness*, where Kirk actually sacrificed himself for everybody already, how do you go on? The time jump was important, because what happens after that? When Kirk thinks about life, what does that mean? How does that reflect on him, and those more subtle, existential issues? With the time we were allowed to have, it helps Kirk in this instance.

STM: What is Kirk's mindset towards this mission, and the Federation, at this point?

JL: That's one of the first thoughts I had, and what I hoped to do when I got together with

A FAST AND FURIOUS CAREER

Born in 1973 in Taiwan, Lin's family immigrated to the USA when he was a child. Growing up in Orange County, California, Lin studied at the University of California, San Diego before enrolling at UCLA to study Film and Television. Graduating from its renowned film school with a Masters degree in Film Directing and Production, Lin already had one feature film under his belt, *Shopping for Fangs*, which he'd co-directed while still studying at UCLA.

His early short films and documentaries soon attracted critical acclaim, and his first solo feature film, 2002's *Better Luck Tomorrow*, premiered at the Sundance Film Festival, achieved numerous award nominations.

It was Lin's third movie however that launched him into the big league, when *The Fast and the Furious: Toyo Drift* became an international box-office smash.

this was the most literal sense. We're taking the *Enterprise* apart. I put a lot of thought into it. We put a lot of effort into it, and it was something that became an inciting incident that was worthy of our characters' potential evolution.

STM: How intensive was it to nail that sequence?

JL: It's interesting, because one of the things I wanted to do on this *Trek* was, in a way, to embrace the old *Star Trek*. Back then, they were shooting on film, and didn't have a lot of budget. Here we had a big budget, but a lot of the

visual effects, especially in sci-fi, have developed into this very smooth aesthetic, and it's kind of losing its humanity. I wanted everything to be as practical as possible. We were building these great crazy rotating sets and gimbles.

What I found out was this is actually the first *Star Trek* where we had shakers on (*hydraulics built into a set to literally shake it – Ed*). I thought, "Wow." I know in the show there was this kind of acting, so I thought they would have used it. It was very important for me to have that kind of tactile interaction.

Lin and Simon Pegg share a joke on set

Simon Pegg and Doug Jung was to figure out a way to deconstruct *Star Trek* and the Federation. Hopefully, by doing that in the movie, we are able to reaffirm why the franchise has been with us for 50 years, and why we still love *Star Trek*, and why it can take us forward another 50 years. That was the first thing I wanted to do on the film.

The other thing is this idea that they're finally now going on their five-year mission. What does that mean? What happens when you have to engage with a new species, and it's great? It's exciting the first or second time. What happens when it's the 400th time? What does that mean to you? Does it lose its purpose? That's something that is very universal. We all go though it, in our own ways. That's something I felt we hadn't seen explored in *Trek*.

STM: It's almost become a rite of passage for directors to destroy the *Enterprise*. How did it feel, shooting that sequence?

JL: Painful. Even though it was my idea, I did not take that decision lightly. Part of the reason behind it was the *Enterprise* might have had different tasks throughout the years, but the *Enterprise* is always there. In a way, it's always been a security blanket. I wanted to take the opportunity to put our characters into situations where they might not be familiar or comfortable, so that we can see how they react, and if they would be able to find their way back to each other. When I talk about deconstruction,

STARRING JOHN CHO

Prior to *Star Trek Beyond*, John Cho (*Star Trek*'s Sulu) had already starred in two of Justin Lin's early films. Cho played Clarence in Lin's 1997 debut movie, *Shopping for Fangs*, and worked with the director again on the multi-award nominated *Better Luck Tomorrow*.

An internet meme in 2016, supporting Asian-American cinema, replaced the stars of numerous famous Hollywood movies with John Cho's face.

STM: The crew gets separated in *Star Trek Beyond*. How important was it for you to delve into Spock and Bones, and really cement that iconic friendship?

JL: I have to be honest. It was one of the treats. Growing up with the show, it was mission-based from week-to-week. Because it was reruns, after you see it a few times, you start thinking of things that were outside of the TV screen. "Wait, they do sleep. They do eat. They do have urges." One of the things I really wanted to do in this one was to see what would happen if we created a situation where Bones was there with Spock, but without Kirk.

STM: What were some of the conversations you had with Idris Elba about his character, Krall?

And... action!

JL: When I was talking about deconstructing *Star Trek* and the Federation, I felt I had to have a character that was going to have a valid opposing philosophy. I also knew this character was not going to have a lot of real estate. I needed an actor that was going to have the strength, that was going to have the presence. Idris was on top of that list. I remember the first time we talked, it was for an hour. I just felt like he totally got it. I feel very fortunate, because I don't know if there are many people on Earth that could pull that off.

Ultimately, it goes beyond good and bad. It's to have quality and perspective that will hopefully have our viewers, at some point, understand that it is a valid philosophy. You might not agree with it – you might actually have feelings for it – but it is a philosophy and point of view.

Lin observes Sofia Boutella doing a spot of voice-recording

STM: One of the compelling things about *Star Trek* villains is that they always have a personal stake in their agendas. Consequently, it causes the crew to examine themselves, and reflect on their purpose, in a different light. How does Krall achieve that, in this instalment?
JL: You see that in the trailers a little bit with the "Frontier pushing back." There's obviously an opposing view that he holds very strongly. We will see that in the movie. Once I'd posed Simon and Doug with that challenge, and we were trying to come up with ideas to deconstruct it, I thought they did a great job of writing and creating Krall.

STM: As a long-time *Star Trek* fan, what was the biggest "pinch me" moment while you were directing?
JL: I don't want this to be a cop-out answer, but it would sneak up on me. I remember walking on the set – and this was before they even lit it – and it was just the hallway set. It was dark. There were still ladders. They weren't done painting it yet. I had this moment where I had to pause for a couple of seconds, because it took me back to when I was a kid, experiencing it from the other side of the screen. Now I'm walking in there, and I'm actually contributing to it.

Because this is not like *Fast and Furious*, where I have an idea and we go and find a location, and put cars on the street – every idea that was in my head was built. I'd say pretty much almost every scene, when I would walk on set, I always had that moment. It happened quite frequently. ⋀

Justin and friends

FILMOGRAPHY
FILMS
Shopping for Fangs (1997)
Interactions (2000)
Crossover (2000)
Better Luck Tomorrow (2002)
Spotlighting (2005)
Annapolis (2006)
The Fast and the Furious: Tokyo Drift (2006)
Finishing the Game (2007)
La Revolucion de Iguodala! (2007)
Fast & Furious (2009)
Fast Five (2011)
Fast & Furious 6 (2013)

TV
Community (2010) (TV)
Scorpion (2014) (TV)
True Detective (2015) (TV)

Justin Lin and Chris
Pine on location

SPACE
THE FINAL
FRONTIER...

STAR TREK: THE STORY SO FAR

Two years into their five-year mission, and in need of some time out, the last thing the crew of the *U.S.S. Enterprise* expected was an encounter with a force from beyond the Federation. Krall's devastating attack sets in motion a chain of events that pushes Kirk and his crew to their limits, and threatens the very existence of the Federation.

But as the *Enterprise* stands on the threshold of galactic events, it is not the first time that the ship and its determined crew have faced seemingly insurmountable odds...

Words: Rich Matthews

Across their entire Starfleet careers, few crews will see as much action as the young Academy graduates stationed aboard the Starship *Enterprise* – and that's before they even set out on their five-year mission to explore strange new worlds, and seek out new life-forms and new civilizations. Fewer still have saved the Earth from destruction – not once, but twice – during their first tour of duty.

Kirk, Spock, McCoy, Uhura, Scotty, Sulu, and Chekov are more than ready to boldly go where no one has gone before, thanks to a series of intense, spectacular events that push them all to the limits of their own capabilities, and beyond. But to look to their future we need to go back to where it all started – in another universe...!

THE KELVIN INCIDENT

It's the year 2387, and a star that is about to go supernova has the potential to wipe out the whole galaxy. A Vulcan plan to detonate Red Matter, to form a black hole that will consume the exploding star, is put into action – but the star explodes shortly before the Red Matter-carrying vessel arrives, destroying the homeworlds of the Romulan Star Empire, Romulus and Remus.

Further destruction is thwarted at the last minute when the Red Matter payload is detonated, but the little Vulcan ship responsible is confronted by a massive Romulan mining vessel, the *Narada*, commanded by Nero – a Romulan hell-bent on revenge for the destruction of his home planets. Both starships are sucked into the singularity, and through a rip in the space-time continuum...

... Over 150 years earlier, the arrival of the *Narada* irrevocably alters the timeline when it destroys the *U.S.S. Kelvin*, along with its heroic first officer, George Kirk. Kirk's wife, Winona, escapes aboard a medical shuttle, while giving birth to the couple's son, Jim.

Growing up in Iowa without his father's guidance, James Tiberius Kirk becomes a cynical rebel who gets caught up in a barroom brawl with a group of Starfleet cadets, after he tries to hit on their fellow student, Nyota Uhura. The fight is broken up by Captain Christopher Pike, who knows who Kirk is, and goads him into joining Starfleet by daring the cocky Kirk to better his father's feat of saving 800 lives in only 12 minutes of command. On the shuttle to Starfleet Academy, Kirk meets Leonard McCoy, a recently divorced fellow cynic who has joined Starfleet as a last recourse. The two immediately become firm friends.

George Kirk (Chris Hemsworth)

The *U.S.S. Kelvin* takes on Nero's fearsome *Narada*, in *Star Trek* (2009)

THE *KOBAYASHI MARU* SCENARIO

Three years later, Kirk finds himself under disciplinary action for cheating on the Academy's *Kobayashi Maru* test – a battle simulation for which there is no winning scenario. Kirk's hearing brings him face-to-face with the simulation's programmer, the half-human/half-Vulcan Commander Spock. However, when Spock's homeworld issues a distress call, all cadets are called up for duty on an emergency rescue mission – all except for a grounded Kirk!

Recognizing similar warning signs that appeared before the destruction of the *Kelvin*, Kirk gets McCoy to smuggle him onto Pike's ship, the *U.S.S. Enterprise*, to warn the captain.

Kirk is stranded on Delta Vega

Kirk (Chris Pine) meets an older, wiser Spock (Leonard Nimoy)

ON DELTA VEGA, KIRK MEETS A STRANGELY FAMILIAR ALIEN FROM ANOTHER FUTURE... AN AGED SPOCK!

Uhura, who speaks Romulan, confirms to Pike and first officer Spock that Kirk is right. The *Enterprise* arrives to find the rest of the fleet destroyed by the *Narada*, which is now drilling through Vulcan's planetary crust. Despite their heroic efforts, they are unable to stop Nero kidnapping Pike, and using Red Matter to take his revenge by destroying Vulcan. While Spock manages to save some of the Vulcan High Council, including his father, his human mother is just one of over six billion casualties.

Kirk and Spock clash over what to do next, and Spock strands Kirk on a nearby ice planet, ordering the *Enterprise* to regroup with Starfleet. On Delta Vega, Kirk meets a strangely familiar alien from another future... an aged Spock!

It was this older Spock's mission to deliver the Red Matter payload in the 24th Century, but his ship was captured by Nero after both vessels were flung backwards through time.

Mind-melding with Kirk, Spock reveals a very different timeline to his young friend, and tells him that to beat Nero, Kirk must fulfill his destiny and take command of the *Enterprise*.

FLASHPOINT IN TIME: THE U.S.S. KELVIN

During the five-year mission of the *Enterprise*, Captain James Kirk has often found himself at the center of historic flashpoints, but it was a pattern set even as he was being born.

When Nero's *Narada* slipped through time in its search for Spock, its first fateful encounter was with the *U.S.S. Kelvin*, whose First Officer was George Kirk. It was at this point that history diverged from its original path, with Kirk Senior valiantly taking command of the ship after its captain was killed during the *Narada*'s attack, and taking on the massive alien vessel, head-on.

Kirk's selfless actions saved many of the *Kelvin*'s crew, who had abandoned ship in escape pods and shuttles, including those of his wife and newborn child, James.

The young Jim Kirk of this new timeline would have trouble reconciling the absence of his father from his life with the heroic legend that had grown up around him. Thanks to the intervention of Christopher Pike, Kirk Junior would eventually take inspiration from his father's sacrifice, and aspire to live up to his memory.

In the original timeline, in which George had continued to serve in Starfleet before eventually resigning his commission to spend more time with his family, Jim Kirk had a close relationship with his father. The result: Jim was inspired by his father's career to enroll in Starfleet, and became a legend in his own right.

Nero (Eric Bana) makes his presence
felt on the *Enterprise* crew

A SERIES OF TERRORIST ATTACKS ON EARTH LEAVES STARFLEET IN SHOCK, AND KIRK BACK IN COMMAND.

FINDING NERO

Kirk and Spock head to a nearby Starfleet outpost, where they encounter out-of-favor engineering genius Montgomery Scott, who – with a little future knowledge from Spock – completes his transwarp equation, and manages to beam himself and Kirk onto the *Enterprise*. On the bridge, Kirk goads Spock into anger, relieves him of duty, and takes command of the ship.

The *Enterprise* goes after the *Narada*, just as it arrives at Earth and deploys its drill. Kirk and Spock beam aboard the *Narada* to rescue Pike, and Spock boards the Red Matter ship, which recognizes him as its pilot. The *Narada* pursues Spock – piloting the Red Matter ship – away from Earth, but the two ships collide, igniting the Red Matter. The resultant black hole swallows up and destroys the *Narada* – but not before Scotty beams Kirk, Spock, and Pike back to the *Enterprise* and safety.

In the aftermath, Kirk is made Captain of the *Enterprise*, Pike is promoted to Admiral, and future Spock tells his younger counterpart that he is leaving to start a new Vulcan colony. The main crew of the *Enterprise* take their stations and head off into the unknown...

HEART OF DARKNESS

In an effort to save an entire race from extinction, Kirk violates the Prime Directive by revealing the *Enterprise* to a pre-industrial civilization on the planet Nibiru, while saving Spock – trapped inside an active volcano – from perishing in a cold fusion detonation.

Returning to Earth, Kirk is excited at the prospect of commanding a five-year mission into deep space, but instead, following his actions on Nibiru, command of the *Enterprise* is stripped from him. Kirk is demoted to First Officer, but a series of terrorist attacks on Earth leaves Starfleet in shock, Admiral Pike dead, and Kirk back in command – tasked with

The Nibirans worship their new god

tracking down the rogue officer responsible, John Harrison.

However, when Kirk and the *Enterprise* crew capture Harrison, they uncover a plot instigated by Starfleet's Admiral Alexander Marcus, designed to incite war between the Federation and the Klingon Empire. "Harrison" reveals he is really Khan Noonien Singh, a genetically-engineered superhuman despot from the 20th Century, who was thawed from cryosleep by Marcus, then blackmailed into doing the Admiral's dirty work – or see the rest of his crew executed while still in their cryotubes.

Marcus is so determined to wage war that he is even willing to endanger the life of his daughter, Dr. Carol Marcus, and fires on the *Enterprise* as both ships hurtle through space at warp speed. Kirk is forced to team up with Khan to infiltrate Marcus' ship, the heavily armed battleship, *U.S.S. Vengeance*, aided by Scotty, who has found his own way to board the *Dreadnought*-class ship.

Meanwhile, Spock contacts his alternate older self, who tells him that Khan was the most dangerous adversary his *Enterprise* ever faced – a fact confirmed when Khan betrays Kirk, kills Admiral Marcus, and takes control of the *Vengeance*. He forces Spock to beam over his sleeping crew, whose cryotubes were hidden inside 72 photon torpedoes, but the Vulcan has secretly swapped the sleepers for warheads, and instead detonates the fully-armed torpedoes, disabling the *Vengeance*.

WHAT LIES BEYOND

However, when the *Enterprise*'s own damaged engines fail, the ship begins to fall toward the Earth's surface. With no other alternative, Kirk enters the warp core to manually repair it – and in the process his body is flooded with lethal radiation. The ship is saved, but Kirk dies.

The *Vengeance* crashes into San Francisco, and an enraged Spock fights Khan on a garbage barge, high above the city. Meanwhile, McCoy discovers that Khan's genetically-altered blood can regenerate newly-dead tissue, so puts Kirk's body on ice, and gets Uhura to beam down and tell Spock that Khan is needed alive.

After a pitched battle, Spock finally defeats Khan and, back on the *Enterprise*,

Khan is no match for Spock's Vulcan rage

Kirk is injected with Khan's blood, saving his life. Khan is returned to cryosleep, and he and his crew are "put in storage."

The newly reunited team set off on their iconic five-year mission to explore the far reaches of space, only to find that the final frontier is pushing back... **∧**

Khan (Benedict Cumberbatch)

FLASHPOINT IN TIME: THE BOTANY BAY

Family, again, played an important factor in another gruesome episode that threatened to alter the course of galactic history.

Starfleet officer Thomas Harewood agreed to terms demanded by a mysterious benefactor, who offered a cure for his daughter's terminal illness. Harewood worked in a secret military installation, hidden deep beneath London's *Kelvin Memorial Archive*. To save his daughter, Harewood smuggled a high-explosive device into the facility, which he detonated after sending a message from his benefactor to the treacherous Admiral Marcus. Harewood gave his life for his daughter's – while taking many more – in the revenge attack, plotted by John Harrison, aka Khan.

Khan had left Earth centuries before, sent into exile aboard a spaceship named *Botany Bay*, with Khan's crew – his family – in a state of hibernation inside 72 cryotubes. The ship was discovered drifting in deep space, and Marcus recognized that Khan would be a useful weapon in his quest to keep Starfleet on a war footing, using Khan's family as a bargaining card – if Khan didn't do as he said, they would die.

In the original timeline, Khan's ship would also be discovered, but not until years later – and by Kirk's *Enterprise*! In that history, Khan attempted to take control of the *Enterprise*, and fell in love with a member of its crew along the way.

Kirk left Khan, his new partner, and Khan's crew on the inhospitable planet Ceti Alpha V, where they would be free to set up a colony. Fate intervened, with a cataclysmic upheaval in the planet's environment hitting Khan's people hard. He blamed Kirk for the many deaths that resulted, including that of his wife, and vowed vengeance against the Starfleet captain.

JAMES T. KIRK

As the brash, inexperienced, but heroic Kirk of 2009's *Star Trek*, Chris Pine had made the role his own by the end of the first reel. *Into Darkness* saw him stretch the character, and his Kirk really earned the captain's chair.

Now, in *Star Trek Beyond*, Kirk faces his biggest challenge yet – self-doubt...

Words: Christopher Cooper

STM: we've seen Kirk develop over the first two movies, growing up – he's something of a reprobate in the first one, and he's getting his act together in the second one – so, where do you feel the character is now, as you come into *Star Trek Beyond*?

CP: The first couple films were, for Kirk, a lot about dealing with the loss of his father, looking up to his second father [Bruce Greenwood's Captain Pike], and taking guidance from him while living in the shadow of the legacy of this father that he never got to meet; the anger he feels at having not met him and known him. Those are all wonderful motivators for Kirk – to try to get noticed, to do a good job, to be the best. And now, ten years or so on, I think those fires have abated, and he's looking for new motivation. He doesn't know what a life in Starfleet is like without needing to prove himself, so it's definitely a more mature Kirk, and that's where we find him at the beginning of the movie.

Justin Lin directs Chris Pine on the set of *Star Trek Beyond*

"I JUST WANTED TO HAVE KIRK GO DARK, LIKE HE DID IN THE ORIGINAL SERIES, IN THAT ONE EPISODE WHERE HE GOES EVIL."

Kirk (Pine) and Chekov (Anton Yelchin) amid the wreckage of the *Enterprise*

STM: You've had a couple of years off from the character, between shooting these movies, where you didn't necessarily think about Kirk, but do your life experiences away from the role feed into the way you play the character?

CP: They do. There's no way for my experiences not to inform how I go about it, and I think the overlap for me and Kirk on this journey is that, when I started out, a lot of it, for me, was about being recognized and noticed, and now, a little bit later on in my career, it has way less to do with that. And, similar to Kirk, you have to find new ways of proceeding in your life – new motivations, new passions, new motivators.

STM: Playing Kirk for the third time, how well do you think you know him now?

CP: That was the great joy of this film, in that I think we have more of a sense of ownership over the parts. With Simon [Pegg] behind the wheel, on writing duties with Doug [Jung], there was a lot more ease, and I think we had a lot more fun.

STM: During the writing of the script, Simon and Doug called you all in at some point, to piece together where your characters might go. How was that part of the process for you?

CP: They definitely wanted to have our input on it. I just wanted to have Kirk go dark, like he did in the original series, in that one episode where he goes evil ["The Enemy Within"], but that didn't happen. I didn't get my wish there. The only thing that I told Simon was that I wanted it to be funny, and I wanted the humor just like we've always had it, but I wanted to make sure that that was protected, and it was.

STM: Does that humorous aspect play into those scenes you share with Anton Yelchin, when Kirk is paired off with Chekov for a little while?

CP: For sure. It was nice playing with Anton. I hadn't really gotten a chance in the previous films to do that much with him, and the energies of the two guys are definitely good fodder for comedy. I love Anton.

STM: You're a famously close cast. When you get back together, how much fun is that? I know you hang out a lot off-set.

CP: It's a lot of fun. We were in Vancouver for most of the shoot, so it was like *Star Trek* film camp. And yeah, we go to dinner most nights, and drink our fair share of wine, and laugh, and end up talking back at my place. We had a good old time.

STM: When you're on the promotional trail for a film like this, touring the world, does it ever feel like a kind of road trip with your pals? Do you get to hang out then too, or is it all a bit of a blur?

CP: Absolutely. You take advantage of the opportunity offered to you, which is a free trip around the world with your friends, so you have a good time.

STM: Do you think Kirk would cope with a promotional tour?

CP: I think he'd probably be a big fan of the hanging out with friends, and not so big a fan of answering questions.

ACTION!

As movie fans might expect after seeing *Star Trek Beyond*'s trailers – and considering the input of director Justin Lin and his previous work on the *Fast & Furious* series – the movie is packed with thrilling stuntwork that sees Chris Pine as Kirk often flying by the seat of his pants...

"I do a lot of stuff on the motorbike in this one," says Pine, "and there were definitely moments, riding over scree and gravel, going pretty fast on a bike that I didn't know all that well, without a helmet... that always freaks me out! I've had to do that a couple times now in my career, which is always scary."

"There's one great explosion moment where Anton and I go flying through the air," Pine continues, "They had us on a harness and a rig, so when we jumped, we flew about 25 feet in the air. That was pretty cool. It was like being on a rollercoaster."

"WE SEE KIRK LONELY, AND KIND OF ALONE IN HIS JOB. WE SEE THE DAILY LIFE ASPECT OF WORKING IN A MACHINE."

STM: Let's talk a little about Idris Elba and his character. He's your second British bad guy in a row. How was it working with him?

CP: Idris is a dominating physical presence. He's 6 feet 4 inches, and a big guy. And has, on top of that, really great acting chops. He was wonderful to work opposite. Really, he's like playing jazz. He was very alive and present, and changing stuff from one take to the next, so it forced me to be on my toes.

STM: Idris has described Krall as "predatory," and Simon and Doug have said that Kirk and Krall are similar in some ways, but the extreme opposite in others, so how would you describe this relationship, and what's the nature of their confrontation?

CP: I think, especially over the course of the three films, the main primary relationship between antagonists and myself are anger, and their relationship to anger, and

> "TO BE A WORKING ACTOR IS DIFFICULT, SO TO BE PART OF SOMETHING LIKE *STAR TREK* IS A RARE, RARE THING. I FEEL PRIVILEGED TO BE A PART OF IT."

how they deal with anger. With Khan, it was about baiting Kirk; with Nero, it was, I think, simply riling up all of the anger that Kirk already had inside him; and I think in this new iteration, Kirk has a better ability to witness his own emotions. He's a little bit more of a mindfulness expert. He can see what's happening to him, and respect the anger that his antagonist is feeling, but I don't know if he gets as swept up in it as he would have before.

STM: The other new member of the cast is Sofia Boutella. She's a very physical actress, she knows how to throw things around, and throw herself around. Did you have to work out to keep up?

ENTERPRISE NCC-1701
CREW MANIFEST

JAMES TIBERIUS KIRK

Rank: Captain
Position: Commanding Officer
Species: Human
Date of Birth: January 4, 2233
Place of Birth: Medical Shuttle 37, *U.S.S. Kelvin*, 75,000km from the Federation-Klingon border; raised in Iowa, USA, Earth.

The youngest captain in Starfleet history, Jim (to his friends) is an inspired tactical thinker, a charismatic leader, and a notorious ladies' man. His early career was also marked by a tendency to rush in where angels fear to tread – some might say that's what makes him a hero.

Kirk was a determined and resourceful Academy cadet, coming top of his Survival Strategies and Tactical Analysis classes, although his desire to win almost scuppered his career at the off, when he "beat" the "no-win scenario" *Kobayashi Maru* simulation by secretly reprogramming the test.

Awarded the Palm Leaf of Axanar Peace Mission of Valor by Captain Stephen Garrovick, for his two academic quarters onboard the *U.S.S. Farragut*, Kirk captains the *U.S.S. Enterprise* on its historic five-year mission into the great unknown. His first contacts with numerous races have earned him a reputation as a diplomat.

KIRK'S FINEST MOMENTS

From wayward youth to commanding officer of Starfleet's flagship, James T. Kirk has lived more than most – and died once along the way. Eventful isn't the word!

- Kirk's dogged determination to follow his instincts, even if it meant disobeying direct orders, was key to foiling Nero's attempt to destroy the planet Earth, and tear the United Federation of Planets apart.
- When Pike fell into the hands of Nero, Kirk stepped up to command, taking the captain's chair as if it had been his all along (*Star Trek* (2009)).
- Kirk broke the Prime Directive (Starfleet's cardinal rule – never to interfere in the development of an evolving species) to save his best friend from dying in the inferno of a volcano.
- When it was the only option left to save his ship, his crew, and millions of lives on planet Earth, Kirk didn't hesitate to enter the dilithium chamber at the core of the warp engine, despite the prospect of almost certain death. Flooded with radiation, Kirk sacrificed his life to restore power to the ailing *Enterprise*. Luckily, Bones was able to revive him, using the genetically engineered blood of the 21st Century renegade, Khan Noonien Singh (*Star Trek Into Darkness*).

"I DON'T BELIEVE IN NO-WIN SCENARIOS."

Kirk (Pine) wants his chair back

CP: I don't really take much time to think about it, because I tend to get overwhelmed by the bigger picture of it all. It's so beloved, and there's some pressure there to do right by the fandom. But man, to be a working actor is difficult, so to be part of something like *Star Trek* is a rare, rare thing. I feel privileged to be a part of it, and happy to be a part of something where the founding charter is about bringing together disparate people to work together, which sounds pretty simple, but it's been hard enough for this planet to wrap our heads around. It's a great story that we tell one another, so I'm very happy to be a part of it.

I love this character, and I love the franchise, but more than anything, I really like going back to work with these people. So as long as they don't turn into assholes overnight, I'll definitely want to come back. △

CP: Sofia comes form a dance background, and danced for years for Madonna. She's physically pretty adept, so there was no mad training I could have done to keep up, at all. But this was a fast and furious [laughs] film-making process, so a lot of the stuff in terms of fight sequences, we were learning close to the day of shooting, so there wasn't much time to prepare for anything other than just working out diligently, keeping bodies in shape and all that.

STM: In your profession, and in the kind of roles you've been playing, I guess you must have to keep yourself pretty fit as it is?
CP: Really, what I've learned now, more than anything, is that I pay less attention to getting all muscly, which is a part of the job, I guess, and more on being able to endure repeated takes over time, which, in this business, ends up really hurting you. So, I try to keep as mobile and limber and strong as possible, instead of just doing dumb barbell exercises. You really just want to make sure your spine can handle the tenth roll down the hill.

STM: *Beyond* is set roughly two years into their five-year mission, and the crew are very tired. How does Kirk react to that? Previously your Kirk was quite inward-looking, in a certain way, and now he's grown into understanding his responsibility toward the whole crew. So, how does that effect things as the movie heads off?
CP: In this [movie] there's a really lovely change of pace – and it's something that I think many fans have always wondered about most franchises: What is it like on the days off, when they're not fighting [evil]? What does it look like when Thor has no one to hit with his hammer? What is he doing? Or when

Batman has nothing to do, what is he doing in his cave? Does he play Monopoly, or does he work out? And this crew, being on this mission for a long time, we see a little bit of the monotony of what it's like to be on a long voyage, away from home. We see Kirk lonely, and kind of alone in his job. We see the daily life of working in a machine, and you become something of a bureaucrat, something of a time-puncher, a card-puncher. That is really the most interesting aspect, at least in the first part of the film, that we've never really seen before.

STM: Kirk is kind of stuck in a rut a little bit?
CP: Absolutely! Stuck in a rut without the motivators of his past, with a crew that he loves, but in a job that he's not sure he's in love with.

STM: So could you see yourself, maybe a few decades down the line, coming back to play Kirk again, facing similar issues? An older Kirk, reflecting on approaching retirement, as William Shatner's Kirk did in his later movies?
CP: That's too far in the future for me to say, but at this point I'd be very interested, sure.

STM: How do you think your Kirk would progress?
CP: Oh man, I have no idea. There's so many different ways for it to go down. I'm interested in the bigger philosophical themes that these stories bring up, so as far as I'm concerned, as long as those are really rich, I'd be very interested.

STM: There's a generation now for whom you are Captain Kirk, and always will be. What does it mean to you to play such a well-loved character, and to have become a part of something so massive?

ONE STEP BEYO

When Paramount Pictures decided on a last-minute change of direction for the 13th *Star Trek* movie, it fell to screenwriters Doug Jung and Simon Pegg (yes, that one) to step up to the plate and pen the next chapter in the voyages of the starship *Enterprise*. *Star Trek* Magazine caught up with both writers in March 2016, to discover more about where the crew are headed in *Star Trek* Beyond. Words: Christopher Cooper

ike Montgomery Scott, the character he so ably inherited from James Doohan for J.J.Abrams' reinvigorated *Star Trek* movies, Simon Pegg is not afraid to speak his mind. Sometimes that can get him into trouble.

"I was famously mis-quoted, or misunderstood at least, before the film started [filming], about the studio wanting to be 'less *Star Trekky*', which sounded awful, and wasn't at all what I meant," Pegg says of one such misadventure. "The studio is very conscious of the fact, and rightly so, that *Star Trek* has a very inclusive story about a very inclusive universe, and that, despite the 50 years of history, we shouldn't assume that every audience member knows *Star Trek* inside out."

That rich history galvanized writers Doug Jung and Pegg into finding new ways to tell a *Star Trek* story, while also providing useful back-up to ensure they were getting things right.

"The difficulty I found was [that] there's such a huge amount of material related to the series, and these characters, so we had to think differently," Jung, Pegg's co-screenwriter on *Beyond*, explains, "How

Uhura (Zoe Saldana)

do we side-step that, how do we go against that trope, or embrace certain things in a way that doesn't feel like a retread? That was by far the harder part of the whole process."

Luckily, there was a wealth of information sources available to Jung and Pegg. "We got tips, and found pieces of information, through people who just love *Star Trek*," affirms Jung, "And if we got a good tip, or a good direction, we'd take it from anyone. We had a really great one from the gentleman who did the alien dialects [for *Star Trek Beyond*]. I put something in about Vulcan physiology that was 180 degrees wrong, and he sent an email with a very elaborate explanation, with references to episodes in the original show, that supported what he was saying, so that was great."

While fans should keep an eagle-eye out for subtle references to the original *Star Trek* television series, Pegg is keen to reiterate that there's something for everyone in the new movie.

"Whenever we watched an episode of the old show, we'd always take down the names of ancillary characters, just so that when we had to come up with names for characters, they would be canon," adds Pegg, "Little things that you wouldn't notice if you were new to this thing, but if you were a real *Star Trek* fan, a Memory Alpha-reading super-fan, you'd be like 'Yes, I get it!'

"The whole writing process was about trying to walk that knife edge between bringing a story that could appeal to someone who just

"*STAR TREK* HAS A VERY INCLUSIVE STORY ABOUT A VERY INCLUSIVE UNIVERSE."
SIMON PEGG

A FORCE TO BE RECKONED WITH
"THIS IS WHERE IT BEGINS, CAPTAIN. THIS IS WHERE THE FRONTIER PUSHES BACK."

Simon Pegg on *Star Trek Beyond*'s villain, Krall, played by Idris Elba:

"Our villain is a very interesting force, and the thing that we didn't want him to be was just out for revenge. The last two villains have been very much driven by revenge. We wanted his motivation to be more complex, and more mysterious. There's not much I can say about him, because we want him to be a mystery. He comes out of nowhere, and shocks the hell out of everybody. His story is one that will be told in the film, but in the build-up to it, it should be known that he is an unknown quantity, and poses a threat not just to the crew, but to the entire Federation.

We worked with Idris [Elba] on the fine details, which was a really productive process. Idris is a great actor, and he's really smart. He was really good at pitching little character details, which we were able to adopt and put in."

A new ship for Kirk and company?
(left to right - Anton Yelchin as Chekov, Chris Pine
as Kirk, and John Cho as Sulu)

Jaylah (Sofia Boutella) in a fight for her life

discovered *Star Trek* on cable, and saw there was
a film of it," continues Pegg, "while at the same
time filling it with things that people who'd been
there on September 7, 1966, will appreciate and
love. There are references in there which are
very, very oblique, and references which even a
casual fan will appreciate. It cannot *not* be full
of that. The DNA of this film is abundant with
acknowledgement of what has gone before, but
it has to be an adventure that someone can sit
down and watch for the first time, without any

prior knowledge. It was a case of trying to
make it buzz."

"IS THAT MUSIC?"

Both Pegg and Jung are lifelong *Star Trek*
fans, and were keen to combine the spirit
of adventure that drove both *Star Trek*
(2009) and *Into Darkness*, with the thought-
provoking plots of the original series.

"I always loved the [episodes] that had
an allegorical sense to them," confirms Jung,
"An episode like 'The Doomsday Machine',
which very clearly has that cold war analogy.
They're making a comment in that episode,
in my interpretation at least, that what we do
now will have lasting effects on the future,
and future generations, in a way that we can't
possibly predict. To me, that's the amazing
power of *Star Trek*." Jung was also interested
in ensuring that, in their entry into *Star Trek*
canon, the human story wasn't swamped by
the spectacle of a Hollywood blockbuster.

"Rather than just taking us into a world
that feels dynamic and interesting, visually
or aesthetically, it's bringing [*Star Trek*] back
to this human aspect," Jung maintains, "that
inherent human desire for exploration and

discovery, that also questions who are we, and
what are we trying to accomplish as a species.
That's something that this crew, and the whole
idea of the *Enterprise*, is constantly coming
up against. They always have to confront that
within themselves, and that was something we
were really trying to mine – the real sweet spot
where you get the bigness, and the adventure,
and the scale, but at the same time bringing it
all back to what it is they are trying to discover
about themselves."

After two movies where the action was
very much centered on a threat to Earth, many
fans wanted to see the *Enterprise* take off on
its five-year mission and seek out strange new
worlds. The writers, too, were keen to do so, but
there were options to consider that would open a
variety of dramatic possibilities.

"The natural step seemed to be 'let's
take them on their five-year mission', but the
discussions were always 'how far?'" reveals
Jung, "Is it a year, is it four years? Is it the end
of the five-year mission, which for a whole host
of reasons seems wrong? We thought the idea
of them being about two years in was kind of
interesting. We really wanted to open up, in a
humorous but also a poignant way, what does

Krall (Idris Elba) – A force from beyond

Kirk (Chris Pine) questions his destiny, in *Star Trek Beyond*

Starbase *Yorktown* under attack

it mean to be locked in a big metal tube for two years, with the same people?"

Pegg further explains their reasoning, saying, "Because we liked this idea of exploring the nature of what a mission like that would do to a crew, we thought 'well let's keep this in real-time, let's make it the same length of time it's been since *Into Darkness*, and send them out into what we call the frontier.'"

"LET'S HOPE THIS DOESN'T GET MESSY."

As Pegg reveals, *Star Trek Beyond* finds the *Enterprise* crew have been keeping themselves busy in the intervening years since their encounter with Khan.

"We get the idea that they've been moving around the galaxy, in a variety of directions, and had encounters with many new lifeforms and new civilizations," says Pegg, "They've got the record for the amount of first contacts that they've made, and the amount of new inductees to the Federation that they've managed to court."

We pick up the adventures of the *Enterprise* crew as they broker a treaty between a planet called Teenax and a planet called Fabona, Pegg explains as he outlines the beginning of the movie.

"They stop off at a prototype starbase, called *Yorktown*, which is a Federation hub on the very, very edge of Federation space,"

he reveals, "It's a place where all the new Federation inductees, or anyone who's in the area and fancies going in and picking up a leaflet, can go and learn about it – Doug and I would get into hysterics, writing about Andorians handing out leaflets like they're at an airport. That's where the *Enterprise* picks up the mission that forms the bulk of the story."

Those three years of in-universe history

> ## "THE NATURAL STEP SEEMED TO BE 'LET'S TAKE THEM ON THEIR FIVE-YEAR MISSION', BUT THE DISCUSSIONS WERE ALWAYS 'HOW FAR?'"
> ### DOUG JUNG

THE SPIRIT OF DIVERSITY
"I KNOW WHY YOU'RE HERE. WHY WE ARE ALL HERE."

Doug Jung on the diversity of the Federation:

"One of the things we tried to do, with the idea of being out on the frontier, was to show the level of diversity that you have out there. We comment on that in a few ways, that idea that there's all types of faces that we see. *Star Trek* has always done that.

It's important to Justin [Lin], it's important to me, it's important to Simon, and to the studio, to really look at all these different faces that we're seeing. And I'm not just talking about Latino, or Asian, or black or white, but the aliens and how they are represented, and that they are all valued in so many ways in that universe. That was something we really tried to keep present. We really wanted to show that idea that they are valued, have a big role, and have acceptance."

allowed Pegg and Jung to explore the main characters, giving them an opportunity to align relationships more closely with the original series.

"One of the things that we were afforded, that we hadn't seen before, is the idea that they had spent a lot of time with each other, and had time to develop these relationships," Jung declares, "You never actually saw some of these characters speak one-on-one with each other. We can all posit that Sulu and Chekov probably had a conversation at some point, about 'What did you do this weekend?' or something, but you never really got a sense of that in the movies, so we said let's assume all that, and cut into the middle of those relationships."

As a consequence, fans will see an advancement of Spock and Uhura's relationship, but also find characters paired together in a way that we haven't seen before. "We were really excited about breaking the [characters] out into relationships that you don't normally see," Jung divulges, "Just by doing that, you gain a greater understanding of who those characters are, because they have time to talk. That was really like a breath of fresh air to write. A lot of times in *Star Trek* the primary crew tends to move as a group – there might be discussion and debate within the group, but they are essentially moving in a group, and we very much went against that."

And it transpires that the nature of the five-year mission has had an effect on the crew. "They're right out at the edge, near a big nebula called the Necro Cloud," says Pegg, "constantly pushing into unknown territory and uncharted space, and they're pretty tired. It's been a very successful, but quite an exhausting three years.

"The thing we really wanted to get to grips with in this movie, that we thought was interesting from the very off, was the effect of long-term space travel," Pegg suggests, "and what that does to inter-personal dynamics, and does to people. They're out there, away from their families, their homes, for a long, long time. We wanted to address how would they feel at this point. We had this idea that they were the

Chekov (Anton Yelchin) and Spock (Zachary Quinto) return

Jaylah (Sofia Boutella)

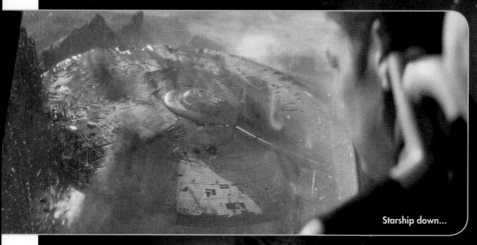

Starship down...

Jung goes into greater detail. "In the broadest sense, one of the things we really wanted to examine was 'What is it that Roddenberry's universe really means?'" Jung expands, "This idea of the utopian vision. Can it exist? Is it a worthwhile aspiration? Are we as a species even capable of it, or is it simply something that invites a never-ending cycle of things knocking us back to the worst parts of ourselves?"

Pegg and Jung realized that Kirk's story would be the ideal prism to explore this idea. "Looking at that through Kirk's point of view can be really poignant," suggests Jung, "At this particular point in his life, he's examining his own reasons for being there, and part of what he has to go through is to recapture his sense of adventure, but with a different definition for himself. I think, as an audience member and definitely as a writer, I find that to be a rich character arc."

"It's about standing by what you believe in, and finding a reason to continue,"

first of the *NCC-17* deep space missions. They were almost like guinea pigs, in a way – no one had ever been out that far, or been out that long before, and we wondered what that would do to them."

"WE WILL FIND HOPE IN THE IMPOSSIBLE."

While *Star Trek (2009)* was about the crew coming together, and *Into Darkness* saw Kirk growing into the role of captain, *Star Trek Beyond* goes further than any previous movie in exploring the ethos of the universe Gene Roddenberry created.

"We chose to slightly question Roddenberry's dream a little bit," Pegg reveals, "and the validity of the Federation projecting a way of seeing things to other people."

> ## "THEY'RE OUT THERE, AWAY FROM THEIR FAMILIES, THEIR HOMES, FOR A LONG, LONG TIME. WE WANTED TO ADDRESS HOW WOULD THEY FEEL AT THIS POINT."
> ### SIMON PEGG

THE ODD COUPLE
"WELL THAT'S JUST TYPICAL"

The teaser trailer included a brief scene between Bones and Spock that evoked memories of their relationship in the original *Star Trek*, and fans can expect more of that in *Star Trek Beyond*.

"We thought it would be nice to send them away together for a while, and to have them butt heads, because they have such opposing views," says Pegg, "At the same time, there's a deep and abiding respect they have for each other, which is marked by this banter – or one-way banter, at least – from Bones to this perplexed, truculent resistance from Spock. We thought it would be really fun to have them exist in the same space, and see what that did, what effect that has on a situation. Doug and I had the most fun writing for those two characters."

"The typical dynamic usually involves Kirk and the sort of 'triangle'," adds Jung, "So you have the emotional represented in McCoy, and the rational represented in Spock, and they're both a little like the angel and the devil on Kirk's shoulder. But in isolating those two, it becomes the greatest odd couple storyline that you could have."

Bones (Karl Urban) supports a wounded Spock (Zachary Quinto)

Red Shirts take a hit

Pegg asserts, "Having the courage of your convictions, and really believing in what you're fighting for. That's the main drive for this one. We really wanted to use this as an examination of the whole story, and take stock. Kirk is at a point in his life where he's outlived his dad, and is thinking 'am I in this for the right reason? Am I doing this because of my father, or am I doing it because I believe in the Federation?' Kirk, Spock and Bones, all of the characters to some degree, think about where they are in the universe, and whether they're on the right track."

"LET'S NEVER DO THAT AGAIN."

With the writing duo focused on exploring the characters, and the very nature of *Star Trek*, how does this third movie relate to the previous outings, in what has become popularly known as the "J.J.verse"?

"Not being a J.J. Abrams movie, it's going to feel slightly different, aesthetically," says Pegg, "and Justin Lin (Director of *Beyond*) brings his own touches to it that make it his own, but it's a continuation of that story. Even though it doesn't say 'previously on *Star Trek*...' at the beginning, it's still very much part of what we set up with the first two films."

When *Star Trek Magazine* spoke to Pegg and Jung, the movie was still some way from being finished, and pick-ups were about to be shot in Los Angeles, but both had seen rough cuts, and were reassuringly pleased with the results.

"It was an early cut, so there's still work

to be done. For me, some of the moments that the characters have are just great," confirms an enthusiastic Jung, "The actors play them so well, and there's that sense of adventure that Justin really did capture. There's stuff in there that's going to be really spectacular.

"This is a *Star Trek* that feels different to J.J's two," Jung continues, "which I don't mean in a bad way, as they're amazing, but it felt like a step forward in the timeline of these characters, and where these particular actors are taking the franchise."

"What I saw was joyful," agrees Pegg, "It was really, really fun, and I was very happy at the end of it. Loads of stuff that we wanted to get into it are right there, including sweet nods to Leonard Nimoy, and various things I know the fanbase are going to appreciate. I've got really high hopes. I watched it on my computer, which is no way to watch a movie like that, but I was really thrilled." ⋀

SPOCK

Returning as cinema's best-loved half-human/half-alien scientist in *Star Trek Beyond*, Zachary Quinto finds new avenues in which to explore Spock – the "emotionless" Vulcan who found love with an emotional Earth girl.

Words: Christopher Cooper

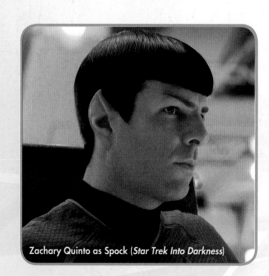

Zachary Quinto as Spock (*Star Trek Into Darkness*)

Star Trek Magazine: I'd like to start, if I may, with the passing of *Star Trek*'s original Spock, Leonard Nimoy, in 2015.

Zachary Quinto: It was, obviously, a really profound loss for me, personally, and I miss him all the time. Everybody really came together and made this movie with Leonard in our hearts, so there's a kind of presence that he had, even in his absence. His spirit was very much a part of this film. I feel like his legacy carries on in many different ways, although it pales in comparison to having him here. It was definitely a bittersweet experience without him. He was an amazing man.

STM: There's something of a tribute to Nimoy in the film. How do you think audiences will respond to that?
ZQ: I think people will see where it's coming from, and it's coming from a place of love. I felt it was very important that we acknowledge it, and I think Simon [Pegg] and Doug [Jung] did a beautiful job of finding a way to fold it in.

STM: Talking of the writers, with the changes behind-the-scenes for this movie, with a different director and writing team, does it feel like a very different *Star Trek* to you?
ZQ: Not entirely, but I do feel it will have its own sensibility as a result of Justin [Lin] directing, and Simon and Doug's script. I feel like it maintains its core, but things are just a little bit different, because of the different people.

STM: What did Justin Lin bring to this movie that differs to the experience of working with J.J. Abrams?
ZQ: Justin came in with a really clear vision for the story he wanted to tell, and a quiet confidence, you know? He's a very different person to J.J.

J.J. is very gregarious and outgoing, and Justin's a little bit [shier]. He came in with this tremendous sense of collaboration, and openness to what we had to say about the characters that we've been playing for this long. He was very respectful of that.

So, it was different. It remains to be seen how people react to it, or what they take from it, but in the experience of making of the movie, I would say that the essence of the franchise, and these people, remains the same, in a lot of ways.

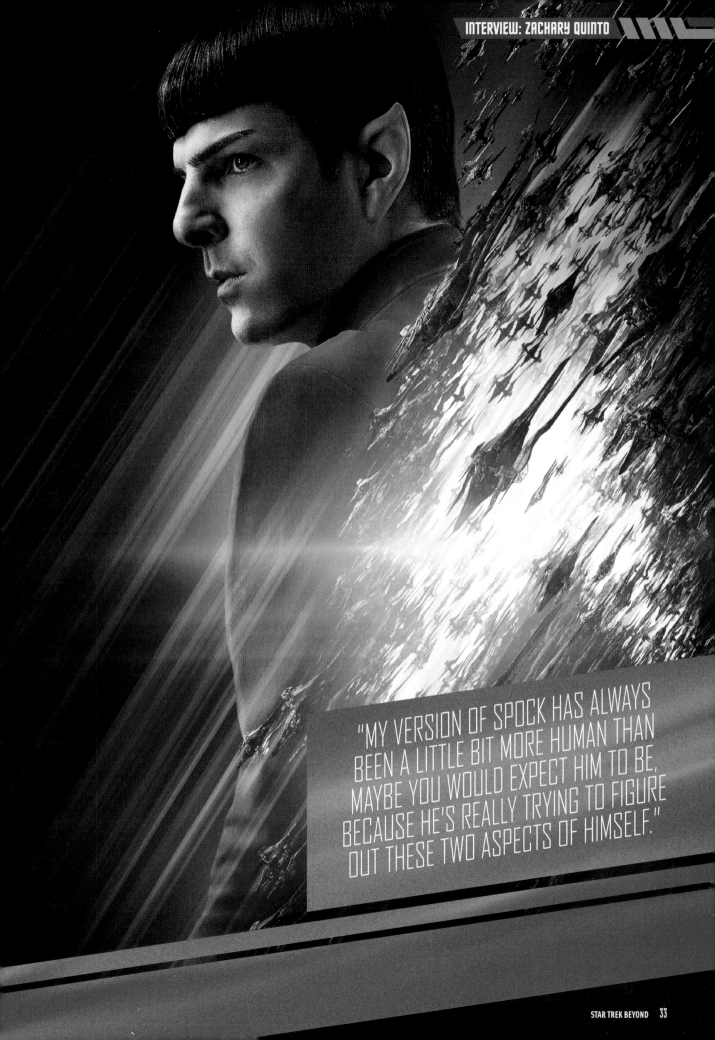

"MY VERSION OF SPOCK HAS ALWAYS BEEN A LITTLE BIT MORE HUMAN THAN MAYBE YOU WOULD EXPECT HIM TO BE, BECAUSE HE'S REALLY TRYING TO FIGURE OUT THESE TWO ASPECTS OF HIMSELF."

Spock (Quinto), Jaylah (Sofia Boutella), and Bones (Karl Urban), go on the offensive

STM: There was also a collaborative input between yourself and the writers, in the development of your character.
ZQ: Having Simon as the co-writer of the film was really great, and exciting for us in a lot of ways but, you know, the part I'm aware of is that it gave us direct access to the stories that we are a part of, and he was really open and interested in what we had to say about that. So, yeah, it was a great sense of, "Let's do this together," and I think the movie reflects that.

STM: Given that *Beyond* is set two years into the *Enterprise*'s five-year mission, has Spock changed during that period?
ZQ: Emotionally, he has definitely evolved since the last time we saw him, but I think he's a little more settled in his human/Vulcan disparity. At the same time, I think he's at a bit of an existential crossroads, and he's trying to determine where his energy would best serve other people. Is Starfleet the path that he should stay on, or is there another? Contributing to the rebuilding of new Vulcan, perhaps that would give him more of a sense of purpose, or more of a sense of accomplishment, even? So, that's where he starts, and things go on from there.

STM: Given Spock's pragmatic, logical nature, how does he respond to Idris Elba's character, Krall, coming from such an oppositional viewpoint to our heroes?
ZQ: I think Spock should have an intellectual understanding of where Idris' character is coming from, but just based on the sheer fact that this position means the slaughtering of innocent people, that prevents Spock from ascribing to any similar kind of beliefs.

STM: On a lighter note, Spock and McCoy spend a lot more time together in this film than they

The logical Mr. Spock

have previously. How was it exploring that classic *Star Trek* relationship, and working with Karl Urban so closely?
ZQ: Well, I love that relationship, and there's so much humor in it. Karl's amazing, and we had a great time working together, so yeah. I like that storyline. I feel like it's refreshing, and it's really rooted in a lot of history for people who are fans of the franchise, from before.

STM: And for fans of your *Star Trek*'s character relationships, have Spock and Uhura moved on in theirs?
ZQ: It has moved on.

STM: Is this one of those circumspect questions that you can't really answer?

"EVERYBODY REALLY CAME TOGETHER AND MADE THIS MOVIE WITH LEONARD IN OUR HEARTS."

ZQ: Yeah, it kind of is. I'm trying to be interesting but vague. I mean, they're always evolving, I would say. Part of Spock's existential crossroads is about his relationship with Uhura, and if it's serving both of them – and if not, then what do they do about it?

STM: So we initially find Spock asking questions of himself. How does that move forward?
ZQ: Well, he immediately gets sidetracked by this catastrophic event that involves the whole crew of the *Enterprise*, and then they are separated from one another. That's when Spock and Bones find themselves marooned together, and Spock gets seriously injured and has to work through that. By the end of the movie he's grateful to be alive, he understands what being alive means in a different way, and I think he understands where his place is. I think, ultimately, he feels like he knows where he belongs; he knows what he needs to do at that point.

STM: What are the challenges of portraying a character who takes a logical approach to his thinking, and supresses his emotions, when you're surrounded by a bunch of characters that are very much emotionally led?

> "PART OF SPOCK'S EXISTENTIAL CROSSROADS IS ABOUT HIS RELATIONSHIP WITH UHURA, AND IF IT'S SERVING BOTH OF THEM – AND IF NOT, THEN WHAT DO THEY DO ABOUT IT?"

ZQ: The trick is to cultivate an inner life that's deep enough to draw in the audience, and make them understand that there's so much more going on than meets the eye. Also, my version of this character has always been a little bit more in that grey zone, between the Vulcan and the human sensibility. That continues in this movie, too. My version of Spock has always been a little bit more human than maybe you would expect him to be, because he's really trying to figure out these two aspects of himself. It's an interesting challenge – certainly a unique one.

STM: With Spock, do you still feel you're cultivating that "inner life," or is it always there for you?
ZQ: With a role like this, there's such a familiarity now. I felt like I was able to drop into this world and explore it as the script allows. It becomes more and more a part of me every time I do it, whereas the first time I was trying to learn all this stuff about the *Star Trek* universe, and figure out the physicality. Now I understand it in a different way, but it's still a process.

The script itself was evolving as we were shooting. We would rehearse scenes and ask questions, or raise concerns, and Doug and Simon would go off and do a little rewrite and bring it back. The process was very organic.

STM: Was that organic approach a positive experience on this movie?

CREW MANIFEST
ENTERPRISE NCC-1701

SPOCK

Rank: Commander
Position: First Officer; Science Officer
Species: Half-Vulcan, half-Human
Date of Birth: 2230
Place of Birth: Shi'Kahr, Vulcan

Logical, loyal, and highly intelligent, Spock was one of the Starfleet Academy's most accomplished and lauded graduates, achieving the rank of Commander by the age of 28.

Following a turbulent childhood on Vulcan, where he faced prejudice due to his mixed parentage (his mother was an Earth human), Spock was set to become the youngest ever inductee into the Vulcan Science Academy. When the Vulcan High Council implied his human half was a "disadvantage" that he had overcome, however, Spock rejected their offer in favor of joining Starfleet.

SPOCK'S FINEST MOMENTS
Known for the Vulcan traits of emotional balance and use of logic, Spock has displayed a tendency to defy both with acts of selfless heroics, love, and anger...

- Ignoring the danger, Spock beamed to the surface of an unstable Vulcan in an attempt to rescue his parents, along with members of the High Council, despite the prejudice they'd shown him years before.
- During the *Narada* incident, and despite their differences, Spock recognized Kirk's qualities as Acting Captain, and stood alongside him when it mattered most, beaming aboard the *Narada* to stop Nero (*Star Trek* (2009)).
- Despite being stranded and facing certain death inside an active volcano, Spock followed orders to set off a cold fusion device (of his own invention) to save the entire Nibiran race.
- Fighting Khan hand-to-hand on automated floating barges, high above San Francisco, an enraged Spock controlled his emotions at the last moment, dragging Khan back to the *Enterprise* to save Kirk's life (*Star Trek Into Darkness*).

"I WOULD CITE REGULATION, BUT I KNOW YOU WILL SIMPLY IGNORE IT."

McCoy supports his injured friend

Spock (Zachary Quinto) raises an eyebrow (*Star Trek Beyond*)

ZQ: Yeah. I would say that Simon, stepping into a leadership position as writer, made us all feel really excited that there was somebody from within that was shepherding our stories. And Justin brought with him a kind of organic energy, making sure that we got what we needed by trusting that we got what we needed. He was really clear and confident about that as well.

I feel like our camaraderie and our friendships feel very organic, and never forced and never manipulated, and I think the ways in which the movie benefits from that are myriad.

STM: Where else would you like to take Spock, were you given the chance to come back a fourth time?
ZQ: I don't know where I'd want to go with it, honestly. I feel like it could go in any number of directions. It depends on where Spock ends up channeling his energy in his future, if there is a future. I could be interested in exploring more of his personal life, maybe, and getting into some explorations of what that looks like.

I tend to stay open to the possibilities, and then be specific about them when it's more of a reality, because at this point there's no guarantee we're going to make a fourth movie, and the only thing that will guarantee making a fourth movie is the third movie doing really well. We have to find out what iteration that movie would be, and then figure out how Spock fits in to it. I love these people; I love my friends that I get to make these movies with, so I would be happy to make another movie with them.

STM: Were there any scenes during filming that you felt were unique on-set experiences that have stayed with you?

ZQ: There's this one set that they built, and it was so massive! Idris Elba's character [Krall] has an operations base, and we spent weeks and weeks working on this set in Vancouver. I've never seen anything like it. It was unfathomably huge, and there was a lot of rain. It was like raining and raining. It was such a very strange part of the shoot, because we'd been inside for the majority of it and then, suddenly, we had three weeks scheduled outside and it just started raining, like it hadn't rained all summer.

I remember being on that set one day, it's pelting down with rain, and just looking around and thinking, 'this is crazy, you're in this place that's like another planet.'

It was kind of indicative of the movie in general, like we're moving into this new territory that's a little bit uncharted, and a little bit unknown, and that moment of just standing in the rain on that giant outdoor set stands out. It wasn't an amazing moment, I wasn't out of my comfort zone or anything, but I just thought, "this is epic level stuff."

STM: Have you ever worked on sets like that before?
ZQ: I've been on a lot of sets, but I've never seen anything quite like that. ▲

ZACHARY QUINTO

Pennsylvania native Zachary Quinto graduated from high school in 1995, having won the Gene Kelly Award for Best Supporting Actor in *The Pirates of Penzance* before going on to study at Carnegie Mellon University's School of Drama. Previously best known for his role as Sylar in *Heroes*, Quinto has since had recurring roles in *American Horror Story* and *The Slap*, and produced numerous short films.
- Adam Kaufman – *24* (2001-2010)
- Sylar – *Heroes* (2006-2010)
- Dr. Oliver Thredson/Chad Warwick – *American Horror Story* (2011-2013)
- John Smith – *Hitman: Agent 47* (2015)

MAKING STAR TREK BEYOND:
THE INTERGALACTIC SEWING BEE
SANJA HAYS: COSTUMES

A blend of the old and the new

Careers, much like life itself, can take unexpected twists and turns.
Pieces fall into place suddenly, opportunities present themselves, and
are embraced or ignored. And, over time, things often come full circle.
All of the above applies to Sanja Hays, costume designer of the Justin
Lin-directed *Star Trek Beyond*.

Words: Ian Spelling

"I went into costume design, I don't want to say by accident, but almost by accident," explains Sanja Hays, costume designer on *Star Trek Beyond*. "I actually graduated with a degree in architecture (from the University of Zagreb), and then I worked as an architect, but I wanted to change things, and an opening came up at the [film] studio in Zagreb, in Croatia, which is where I was born. They offered me a position to be an intern, an assistant in the costume department, just after I graduated college.

"To me, anything with the movies would have been great, because I was always watching every movie that came out. It was between costume design and production design, but costumes had an opening and I was like, 'Great.'"

Her career really took off when she married and moved to the USA, leading to her first brush with *Star Trek*. Looking back at her experience on the movie *Star Trek: Insurrection*, Hays sums it up in a single word: "Crazy."

"First of all, I was a huge Trekkie, always. *Star Trek* was something we all watched," she reveals, "I guess we were all nerds, but it was huge. My agent was able to get me an interview for that, and to say that I was excited doesn't even begin to describe it. I went to my interview with a whole bunch of books and samples, and pictures and fabrics. I actually had a little shopping cart with me, and when I walked in they laughed at me. There were some big names [competing for the job], actually, but they went with me, even over my mentor at the time, Joseph Porro. I got the job. I guess they liked my enthusiasm."

BACK TO BAK'U

Hays conferred upon the primary alien race in the movie, the Bak'u, (and especially Anij, played by Donna Murphy), their earthy, almost hippie-esque appearance. She also devised the intricate appearance of the Son'a, particularly Ru'afo (F. Murray Abraham), and his alluring nurses. "I think that I tried to push the envelope in every single direction," Hays recalls, "Maybe because I'm an architect, I try not to stop at fabric. I always like to go beyond. One thing that was interesting was the nurses had these latex suits. When I first proposed them to the producers and director (Jonathan Frakes), they were like, 'Oh my God.' It was kind of risqué for *Star Trek*, right? But when they saw it, when they saw the drawings, and saw what they looked like [in the costumes], they liked it. So we made the suits for these futuristic attendants out of latex, and we sprayed them with this ballooning to enhance their curves. They were, in the end, very, very happy, but at the time it was very much pushing the envelope of *Star Trek*."

"MAYBE BECAUSE I'M AN ARCHITECT, I TRY NOT TO STOP AT FABRIC. I ALWAYS LIKE TO GO BEYOND."

Now, nearly 18 years later, Hays is back in the *Star Trek* universe, creating the costumes for *Star Trek Beyond*. Hays had collaborated with director Lin frequently in the recent past, including on *The Fast and the Furious: Tokyo Drift*, *Fast & Furious*, *Fast Five* and *Fast & Furious 6*, as well as the pilot episode of the television series, *Scorpion*, which Lin directed.

Hays laughs as she admits that she thinks Lin knew she served as costume designer on *Star Trek: Insurrection*, although she isn't entirely sure whether that's the case.

"Justin and I are quite close," she says, "We'd done all of these *Fast and Furious* movies together, and I really consider him a friend. I assume he knew, but I don't know if that is the reason why he brought me on (for *Star Trek Beyond*) or not. I never did ask him that. Justin is a very thorough man, though, so I'd suspect he would know, because he's on top of everything."

COMMAND

ENGINEERING

SCIENCE

A CUT ABOVE AND BEYOND

Sanja Hays moved to the United States from her native Croatia after marrying boom operator and sound mixer John Hays, whose credits include *Dexter* and *Looper*, as well as *The Albatross* – a film John Hays wrote and directed, with Sanja Hays producing.

Her career began in earnest in the late 1980s, when she worked as an assistant to costume designer Joseph A. Porro on such films as *The Blob*, *Tombstone*, *Stargate* and *Independence Day*. Later, venturing out on her own, Hays served as costume designer on a wide array of movies and TV shows, among them *Blade*, *Star Trek: Insurrection*, *Cheaper By the Dozen*, *Mission to Mars*, *The Mummy: Tomb of The Dragon Emperor*, *Total Recall* (the remake), *Battle: Los Angeles*, *Sleepy Hollow* (the pilot and one other episode of the Bad Robot production), and *Scorpion* (the pilot, produced by *Star Trek Into Darkness*' Roberto Orci, and directed and co-produced by Justin Lin). Additionally, Hays served as costume designer on *Maze Runner: The Scorch Trials*, and all seven entries in the blockbuster *Fast and Furious* franchise.

"I WAS A HUGE TREKKIE, ALWAYS. *STAR TREK* WAS SOMETHING WE ALL WATCHED."

BACK ON BEYOND

So what was Lin's mission statement to Hays, as he set about pre-production on *Star Trek Beyond*? What did he need her designs to put across on screen?

"There were a few things that were important to him," Hays replies, "But most important to him – and I think it's going to reflect in the whole movie – was to keep the essence of *Star Trek*, to keep everything that was great about *Star Trek*, and then go and push it forward. So, with the costumes, we went one direction with the uniforms, and we've almost pulled it back more to the original, because he felt that, if he was going to push the movie in a little bit of a different direction, then we have to visually keep the essence close to home.

"If you've seen the photos and trailers from *Star Trek Beyond*, you see that I tried to keep the main cast's costumes more like the originals, but with the new fabrics and the new technology that have developed," Hays continues, "Then, with the other elements, we wanted to make it different, to go with the times, to go with the technology as it happens, with the way the taste of the audience changes, and all of that. So, the rest of the costumes, for the other characters, were pushed forward and made differently."

STRANGE AND HEROIC

A perfect case in point were Hays' designs for Krall, as played by British actor Idris Elba.

"Justin wanted you to look at Krall and not be sure whether it's him or an armor, where the man within starts and stops, and he wanted you to not be sure how he changed, and what really happened with him," Hays notes, "Justin wanted us to create something you hadn't seen in previous *Star Trek* movies, or previous sci-fi movies. The other big one was Jaylah, played by Sofia Boutella, and I think that's probably one of the most successful we've done, Joel Harlow and myself. She's an alien woman who needed to look interesting, and strange, but also heroic.

"And, of course, the thing every *Star Trek* movie has to show is the diversity of the universe," Hays adds, "So, with the extras, we tried to show how diverse *Star Trek*'s universe is. With this movie, like he does in his other movies – Justin's big dream, I would say – is to go with the diversity and equality of race and gender, and all of that.

Hays also embraced the opportunity to address a problem she'd had with *Trek*'s uniforms in the past. "Oh, yes, there was one more thing, something that Justin hadn't requested, but that always bothered me in previous *Star Trek*s," she says, "that many of the uniforms didn't have pleats, didn't have length. They were these cute, sexy things, which were great, but they didn't have pleats. I was really bothered by it. So we changed that, and I think there was a really positive response from Zoe (Saldana), of course, and, from the audiences that have seen it."

KRALL

A heroic new costume for Chris Pine as Kirk

THAT JACKET

Another costuming element worth touching on is the nifty new jacket that Captain Kirk (Chris Pine) wears for much of the proceedings. It's blue, with yellow and silver mixed in, and it accentuates Pine's steely blue eyes beautifully, which was very much the goal.

"The inspiration for those jackets was Kirk is going to another planet," Hays reveals, "They have these escape pods, and a survival suit in the pods that can help you survive in any environment you encounter. The script went through some changes, but that was the idea behind that, that they get in some different suits, escape in the pods, and go on to a different planet. But, aesthetically and costume-wise, the idea was, in my mind and in Justin's mind, to make Chris look really heroic, like a cool leading man. Because he's such a gorgeous guy, I saw him as almost like a space cowboy. So, for me personally, I just wanted to do justice to him, and make him look as good as possible, because he's such a charismatic man, while still having it make sense for the movie. So it was created for Chris, and then Anton (Yelchin) wore it. Anton looked great in it too, really good."

Many *Star Trek* fans take their *Trek* super-seriously, and find ways of weaving it into their daily lives. In the near future, in the real world here on Earth, it would surprise no one to see fans cosplaying, trick or treating, or simply attending *Star Trek* conventions dressed in *Star Trek Beyond* costumes, especially as Captain Kirk in that jacket, or as Krall or Jaylah. Those fans may make the costumes by

hand, starting from scratch, and motivated by Hays' achievements. Mention that possibility to Hays, and this most-effusive, talkative woman suddenly finds herself at a loss for words.

"It's amazing," she enthuses, "It's just amazing. I don't know what else to tell you. You know, as a designer doing something like *Star Trek*, it's more than a movie. I'm very happy, and very proud of what we have done, all of us, together."

TEAM EFFORT

Hays ultimately toiled on *Star Trek Beyond* for "nine months, six days a week, 14 hours a day." Of course, she didn't do it alone, and she warmly credits her crews in both Los Angeles and Vancouver, who helped "translate" her ideas from concepts to camera-ready costumes. "They were fantastic," she says, "I couldn't have done it without them."

What's next for Hays remains to be seen. She doesn't have a subsequent job lined up, or at least not one she can announce just yet. However, she makes no bones about the fact that she'd welcome the opportunity to contribute to *Star Trek* again, and she hopes it's not another 17 years before she gets the opportunity to do so.

"*Star Trek Beyond* was just the most amazing experience, one of the best experiences," Hays concludes, "So I would love it. I loved working with Justin, but I equally loved working with the whole J.J. (Abrams) crew. This whole group was great. It was amazingly huge, but amazingly rewarding. So, yeah, I would take another *Star Trek* film without the slightest hesitation." ▲

A lot of rewarding hard work went into creating the looks of characters such as Krall in *Star Trek Beyond*

UHURA

Getting the emotionally repressed Spock hot under his Starfleet collar can't be easy, but Zoe Saldana's dynamic Nyota Uhura knows how to push his buttons – and keep him in his place. But how is their relationship holding up to the rigors of the *Enterprise*'s five-year mission?

Words: Bryan Cairns

Will Spock and Uhura's love survive the final frontier?

Star Trek Magazine: Back in 2009, all eyes were on the *Star Trek* reboot. How did it feel reuniting with this cast for your third outing?
Zoe Saldana: I'm just happy we were able to bring the entire cast back. We started a magical thing with *Star Trek* in 2009. I can't imagine experiencing all this without Chris, Zach, Karl, John, Anton and Simon. I was so happy to be back with the team.

STM: It's been a while since *Star Trek Into Darkness* was released, back in 2013. Stepping back on set, what had you missed the most about Uhura?
ZS: I missed how different she is, and how important it is for her to do her job well. I missed how diligent she is. She cares. I also like that every installment that I came back to, Uhura and Spock are evolving, they're in a different stage. We definitely take it further in this installment.

STM: The Uhura/Spock romance has been a real highlight of the movies. What have you enjoyed about how it's been developed?
ZS: It just became human. If you are going to have a group of people working together, and traveling together for years, you need to allow humanity to set in. People will fall in love. People will become very, very close to each other. I like that the writers gave Zach and me an incredible subject and story to build upon. That's what we've been doing.

STM: The two have experienced some hiccups in their relationship. Where do they stand now, and in what ways does *Beyond* further explore that dynamic?
ZS: Their dynamic has taken a turn for the better. All of the crew are tested in this movie, but they all stick together. Spock and Uhura's friendship is going through the biggest test. I feel like they are going to pull through.

STM: Sequels should never simply recycle and spit out previous material. How is *Beyond* different to the first two installments?
ZS: I don't think they compare. We have raised the bar in this third one, just as they raised the bar in the second one. There's a bad guy, for

"UHURA AND SPOCK ARE EVOLVING. THEY ARE IN A DIFFERENT STAGE. WE DEFINITELY TAKE IT FURTHER IN THIS INSTALLMENT."

Uhura (Zoe Saldana) is taken prisoner by Krall's forces

sure. The *Enterprise* is going to be threatened on a much larger scale. They are going to have to find a way to make it back and save the galaxy.

STM: Simon Pegg co-wrote the script. Do you feel that being part of the cast gave him a unique perspective on this franchise?
ZS: I think Simon has been a fan for a long, long time. He was really excited and super-nervous to do this. We loved his script, we really did. Simon is a writer and a filmmaker who's known for creating very entertaining movies, with heartfelt stories and characters. And humor is the weapon that he uses to seduce and charm and unite. There's a lot of that there. But it doesn't become a comedy at all. He allows the characters to breathe and relax.

STM: This is a long mission, and the characters are asking deep personal questions about themselves. What's troubling Uhura at this point in her life?
ZS: I'd say what's troubling her in the beginning is Spock. Spock always makes her worry. What ends up being the biggest concern is the same for everybody – it's having to stay alive, and stop this villain from destroying us all.

STM: How does this movie's villain, Krall, stack up against previous adversaries Nero and Khan?
ZS: I really liked this character, Krall. I like what he's about. He also represents a lot of individuals in the past 10 to 15 years. When it comes to terrorism, we are pursuing a lot of meaningless targets. Then [you ask], "What is it like to be a negative recipient of someone's personal vendetta?" Those are people who are not uncommon in the *Star Trek* universe. This villain is different from Eric Bana's character [Nero], he's different from Benedict Cumberbatch's character [Khan], a very lethal Big Bad – and, the make-up is astounding!

STM: Uhura and Sulu get paired up a lot in this movie. How do they get along?

ZS: They get along very nicely. That's one thing I love about Uhura, that she doesn't argue with anyone. It's, "What do you need next? What needs to be done? Let's get the hell out of here." She's done just that. Having to depend on each other, that's true friendship. That's when you realize they're made for each other. That's what I love about this group of individuals together.

STM: John Cho has a reputation for being the resident joker of the cast. How did he keep things light on the set?
ZS: He did different impersonations. He would also ask the women what they think he should eat, because John feels he should be watching what he eats. He does things like that. There are times when he doesn't smile at all, and that makes everyone around him laugh. John is very funny. But as soon as the director yells, "Action!" he transforms back into Sulu, and does his work so beautifully and gracefully. Then, as soon as we are prepped and break, he puts his character to the side and starts joking around the set. There's a lot of love in his spirit.

STM: One of the film's other themes is diversity within the Federation. With that in mind, what are your thoughts on being the female lead in a male-dominated cast?
ZS: When I was young and super-unaware, I used to say, "I love being the only girl." I hate it now. It's really lonely. I want to see more women around me. I want to have colleagues that are female. I want to see women conquer and succeed. I want to see more female characters around me, too. I don't want to be the only one. I admire the brotherhood that men have, how they collaborate, and how great they feel when they know they are all in the same room, working for the same project. I want to feel that way with my sisters. I want to feel that way with women.

STM: *Star Trek Into Darkness* had Alice Eve.
ZS: We have an addition to this film's cast too, Sofia

"I WAS THRILLED ABOUT JUSTIN LIN GETTING THIS OPPORTUNITY, AND BEING ABLE TO SHOWCASE HIS WORK."

Boutella. She's phenomenal. It was amazing to have her as part of our team, on- and off-camera.

STM: How was it not having J.J. Abrams' fingerprints on this production?
ZS: We missed him, but we knew he was super-involved. Bad Robot [Abrams' production company] was around. J.J. would email us going, "The dailies are looking great. I'm super-excited." From my end, I missed him, but I was thrilled about Justin Lin getting this opportunity, and being able to showcase his work. I've been a fan of Justin's for a very long time. I've wanted to see him do more.

STM: Directors can make or break a project. What was your initial impression of Justin, and how did he do?
ZS: Justin was the same from the first moment I met him. He is dedicated. He works harder than anybody that doesn't sleep. He barely has any time to crack jokes, but if you want to crack a joke around him, he will appreciate the laughter. He's very responsible, committed and knows what he wants. To feel that confidence in your director, it kind of removes half of the work. You just have to allow yourself to be directed, and that's what he did.

STM: A few things have been tinkered with. The *Enterprise*'s aesthetic has been tweaked. The uniforms have been slightly altered. How pleased were you with some of the changes?
ZS: They feel great. They felt fresh. I certainly didn't feel like we had gone too far away from the original concepts that already existed in the show, or that we created in the first two instalments. It felt youthful, and really wonderful.

> "I WANT TO HAVE MORE COLLEAGUES THAT ARE FEMALE. I WANT TO SEE WOMEN CONQUER AND SUCCEED."

STM: Your résumé includes *Star Trek, Guardians of the Galaxy, Colombiana, Takers, The Losers* and *Avatar*. When did you realize you were the go-to girl for such fierce roles, and what has it meant to you to be part of some of Hollywood's biggest franchises?
ZS: I couldn't have planned it better. If I had planned this, it would never have worked out. I am in love with science fiction, and I love action movies. I was tired of waiting to see female superheroes and action heroes, so I had to become one. This is a calling of mine that I embraced in the first stages of my career. Then, I wanted to explore other kinds of characters, but I'm happy that I didn't, because I know there are a lot of women out there, a lot of little girls, that need these role models. I took the role responsibly, super-consciously, and quite happily.

STM: With all those genre credits, you are basically Comic-Con royalty.
ZS: Yes! I can't wait to go this year! ⌃

ENTERPRISE NCC-1701
CREW MANIFEST

NYOTA UHURA

Rank: Lieutenant
Position: Communications Officer

Species: Human
Date of Birth: 2239
Place of Birth: East Africa, Earth

Nyota Uhura is an ambitious, headstrong, and deep-feeling Xenolinguistics specialist. Proficient in 83 percent of United Federation of Planets languages and regional dialects, her translation skills have proved invaluable during the *Enterprise*'s five-year mission.

Graduating with honors from the Institute for Advanced Mathematics, Uhura was an Academy aide to Commander Spock on the Advanced Phonology and Advanced Acoustical Engineering courses at Starfleet Academy. Their subsequent romantic relationship has been put under strain during various dangerous missions aboard the *Enterprise*.

UHURA'S FINEST MOMENTS
Opening hailing frequencies is about much more than placing intergalactic phone calls, as Uhura has proved on numerous occasions...

- Uhura identified and translated a Klingon transmission revealing that an unknown Romulan ship – Nero's *Narada* – had attacked and destroyed an entire fleet of Klingon ships.
- There was no doubting Uhura's communication skills when she stood up to her superior officer (and lover), Spock, to ensure she was posted to Starfleet's flagship, the *U.S.S. Enterprise*. After demonstrating her fluency in all three Romulan dialects, Uhura was immediately promoted to Communications Officer on the *Enterprise* by Captain Christopher Pike (*Star Trek* (2009)).
- In an attempt to secure their help in finding the terrorist "John Harrison," Uhura negotiated with a unit of Klingon warriors face-to-face, in their native Klingonese dialect.

- Uhura's technical adeptness enabled contact with Old Spock, even though the *Enterprise* was far beyond normal communications range (*Star Trek Into Darkness*).

> "I SURE HOPE YOU KNOW WHAT YOU'RE DOING... CAPTAIN!"

PREPARE
OMA

A FAN'S-EYE VIEW OF THE

The unique, crowd-funded, charitable organization, Omaze, has gained a well-deserved reputation for supporting numerous worthy causes worldwide, by offering once-in-a-lifetime experiences as prizes in return for affordable donations.

Images courtesy of Omaze

TO BE ZED

STAR TREK BEYOND SET

In 2015, Omaze teamed up with Paramount Pictures, Bad Robot, and the cast of *Star Trek Beyond*, to create the *To Boldly Go* campaign, offering an incredible experience to one lucky group of *Star Trek* fans. This is the story of one fan's very special day...

TO BOLDLY GO
CREW MEMBER

Audrianna Davis
Omaze - Star Trek

Words: Audrianna Davis

Zachary Quinto and Karl Urban lend their support

VOYAGE TO VANCOUVER

I honestly didn't believe it at first, but once the words sunk in, I found myself shouting with joy. My parents were so concerned, they actually ran upstairs. When I told them I'd won, they also freaked out, and my mom couldn't help flashing a thumbs up at the webcam. They knew how much *Star Trek* means to me, and were completely overjoyed that I had won!

I have honestly never won anything before, so it was truly unbelievable. The funniest part was when the video went up, announcing me as the winner. It included clips from my interview, and you can really see how shocked and excited I was. My favorite YouTube comment on the video is "I think Audrianna is excited. I'm not sure. It's hard to tell." I laughed over that for days.

Over the next few months, as the other winners were announced, I waited for the day

When I first heard about the Omaze *To Boldly Go* contest, I just knew I had to enter. Not only was it an opportunity to support some truly incredible charities, but the prizes that were up for grabs made it a chance I couldn't pass up.

I told my mom I'd dropped the money on the entry, and was immediately chastized for spending it, what with my first round of student bills looming. She's a *Star Trek* fan, though, so the first thing she asked me was "Are you taking me, if you win?" I laughed, and told her I'd be taking one of my best friends, Summer, along with me. "Well, you won't win anyway!" mom replied, but it was good-natured, because she knows that Summer and I are *Star Trek* soulmates, and we absolutely would have to take that journey together.

I was on my lunchbreak at work, only a week after I'd entered, when I had an email from Omaze. They wanted to do a Skype call with me that evening. The rest of the workday was almost

impossible to get through, but I made it home, and tried to calm down enough so that I wouldn't look or sound too ridiculous.

The interview was really chill, and I was given the opportunity to talk about how much I truly love *Star Trek*, and how it's changed my life. Honestly, the reason Summer and I are as close as we are is because we bonded so much over the most recent film. I come from a family of *Trek* lovers and, when *Star Trek Into Darkness* was released, I truly fell into the *U.S.S. Enterprise*-shaped spiral that my parents claim was my "birthright."

Star Trek spoke to me with its message of a beautiful and prosperous future through equality, human ingenuity, and the spirit of discovery. It very quickly became one of the most important things in my life. When Omaze asked what it would be like to visit the set of the next *Star Trek* movie, all I could say was that it would be a dream come true. To that, they responded with, "You don't have to dream, because you won!"

we would leave for Vancouver to arrive. I had never been out of the country before, so it was a pretty cool adventure to head to Canada. I flew out from Denver at 6am, and met up with Summer at Vancouver Airport. She was coming in from Connecticut, and the trip was extra exciting since we hadn't seen each other in a while. We wore matching T-shirts we'd given each other for Christmas the previous year. It was pretty freakin' adorable.

We arrived at the hotel in the early afternoon, and were welcomed by the wonderful Omaze crew. They had adorable gift bags waiting for us that included our crew badges, and some stuff that would make our day outside the following day a little more comfortable. We took our stuff upstairs to our room, to get settled in while we waited for the other winners to arrive, and had to take a moment to freak out a little about where we were.

BEYOND CHARITY

Star Trek Magazine spoke to Ryan Cummins, co-founder of Omaze, soon after the first *To Boldly Go* winners (including Audrianna) were announced, and asked what inspired Omaze to join forces with *Star Trek...*

"Zachary Quinto (Spock) is a big supporter of *Direct Relief*, so he initially raised the idea of doing an Omaze campaign to benefit the cause," Cummings reveals, "Paramount and Bad Robot knew this would be an opportunity that the other castmembers would love to be part of, given their charitable histories, and offer a fun way to engage fans and supporters around a philanthropic initiative. None of this would have been possible without everyone's participation, the fans included.

"The *Star Trek* franchise is truly global," says Cummings, acknowledging that the *To Boldly Go* campaign received donations from fans in over 100 countries, which he sees as "a testament to the far-reaching nature of *Star Trek*'s community, as well as to their charitable nature. It's inspiring how quickly everyone mobilized to launch this campaign to benefit nine remarkable causes having an impact around the world."

Cummings is unequivocal about Omaze's mission statement, and their plans for the future. "Our higher purpose as a company is to serve world changers," he explains, "We are continually looking to collaborate with studios and production companies as innovative as Paramount and Bad Robot, who recognize the opportunity to leverage these properties to have an even greater impact on the world. To see all that collaborative effort paying off, through the positive response of such a good-hearted and passionate base of fans and supporters, just makes you want to dance on the bridge!"

Words: Christopher Cooper

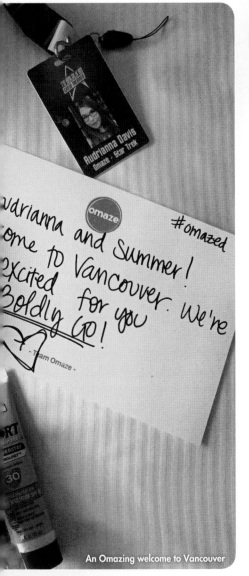

An Omazing welcome to Vancouver

"IT'S SO COOL THAT *STAR TREK* AND OMAZE WERE ABLE TO FORGE FRIENDSHIPS BETWEEN PEOPLE WHO MAY NEVER OTHERWISE HAVE MET."

JOINING THE CREW

The rest of the *To Boldly Go* crew, including the grand-prize winner, Adam Horwitz, were all wonderful. We all got along right away. It was amazing meeting people from all walks of life, from all over the country, who all loved *Star Trek* as much as we did. One winner and her friend came all the way from Ireland, and another brought his 12-year-old daughter along. We had an amazing dinner together, and spent the evening getting to know each other and talking about what we love most about *Star Trek*, before heading back to the hotel to get some rest ahead of our big day.

The next morning, Omaze had breakfast and coffee waiting, and we were briefed for the day. We already knew that we would be taken somewhere outdoors, so we were ready for a long day of hiking around in the sun as we hopped onto the small bus that would take us to the set. We spent the ride talking about what we

Audrianna Davis

The cast of *Star Trek Beyond* pose for an intergalactic selfie

LAST CHANCE TO JOIN US
RESISTANCE IS FUTILE.

#ToBoldlyGo

omaze

were most hoping to see, and it was only around an hour before we arrived at a massive quarry, outside of the city. It was truly incredible to drive up to a movie set that massive. Even from a distance, we were able to see the massive crane that was used to move the giant green screen that would block out the sun wherever they needed it, but the coolest thing was driving up past all the trailers and tents, and all of the extras in costume, as we made our way down to the set proper.

Right away we were greeted by an Assistant Director, who took us on a walking tour through the multiple sets that had been built in the quarry. The scale of everything was incredible. We got to climb through different areas, and learn how everything was crafted. As a movie buff, it was especially cool to see movie magic in action. It was amazing being on sets that would be key locations in the film, and we couldn't help but try and piece together what we thought the plot might be.

ACTION

After getting a chance to see everything in the area, we were taken to our own private tent so that shooting could begin. We were given special headsets and monitors, so we could watch and listen to everything they were doing. We were told that the scene we were watching was a pivotal moment in the film, which made it extra cool. We loved being able to see the subtle differences in each take that they shot, and it

was fascinating to listen in on the directions from director Justin Lin, and hear the discussions between the cast members over what they should try next. We must've seen the same scene shot at least a dozen times, from a dozen

"WE HAD A LOT OF FUN WATCHING ADAM RUN AROUND SET IN HIS SPECIALLY MADE STARFLEET UNIFORM. HE WAS A TOTAL NATURAL!"

different angles, but it never once was boring. We had a lot of fun watching Adam run around set in his specially made Starfleet uniform, and it was a blast watching him on camera. He was a total natural! The whole crew was cheering him on the entire way.

Between takes, we were visited by members of the crew, who would show us different things from the production. First we met with the make-up designer Joel Harlow, who brought several actors in alien prosthetics for us to meet. It was incredible to see them up close, and it was hard to believe there were actually people

CRAFT SERVICES

We broke for lunch around mid-day, and were pleased to learn that we would get to eat at craft services, with the rest of the cast and crew. The food was amazing, and it was extremely cool to get that authentic, on-set experience. We were introduced to everyone by the film's producer, Jeffrey Chernov, and received generous applause. While eating, I even got to sit next to the costume designer for the film (Sanja Hays), which was a real treat. It was really interesting to learn more about the material and the process that goes into designing costumes for film.

This could be you!

"THE REST OF THE TO BOLDLY GO CREW, INCLUDING THE GRAND-PRIZE WINNER, ADAM HORWITZ, WERE ALL WONDERFUL. WE ALL GOT ALONG RIGHT AWAY."

Audrianna with "*Star Trek* soulmate," Summer

underneath the make-up. They were so lifelike. The actors were extremely fun to talk to as well. Some of them were up at absurd hours of the morning to get their make-up on, yet they were still so energetic, and ready to take on the full day ahead of them. That's commitment to a job!

We were also joined by co-writer Doug Jung, which was an incredible opportunity to learn more about the direction this third movie would be taking. As a die-hard *Star Trek* fan, it was amazing to hear what he was able to tell us, and I just knew that they were giving us the movie that fans have wanted for years. We were also joined by the props director, who talked a lot about how the prop weapons were made, and even let us hold them.

Touring the *Beyond* set

John Cho and Zoe Saldana
support the cause

"WHEN OMAZE ASKED WHAT IT WOULD BE LIKE TO VISIT THE SET OF THE NEXT *STAR TREK* MOVIE, ALL I COULD SAY WAS THAT IT WOULD BE A DREAM COME TRUE."

For the second half of the day, we spent our time watching more scenes being shot, and were joined by some of the extras. It was really cool to be able to talk to them about their own experiences on set, and a lot of them were just as big *Trek* fans as we were. Our time on set was drawing to a close, but before we left we met Zoe Saldana (Uhura) and John Cho (Sulu) as they wrapped up for the day. Both of them made sure to thank us for our donations, and were so incredibly kind. We got pictures and hugs before they had to take off, and we had to board our bus home.

BEYOND EXPECTATIONS

We figured that the day was over, and the Omaze team sure had us believing it. If the day had ended right then and there, we would have still been the happiest fans in the world, but there was more to come. As the bus took a little detour on our way back to the hotel, we were told that we had to stop at the studio lot to pick up our phones – but we knew something was up when we were asked to get off the bus...

We were led into a studio building, and were surprised to find a designer and the set of a starship waiting for us. We were taken inside, where we sat in every chair, pushed literally every button and pulled every lever, and combed through the blueprints for the design. It was fascinating, and especially exciting to have our pictures taken in the captain's chair. We couldn't help but wonder just what role the ship would play in the final film.

Just as we were exploring, we were joined by some surprise guests. When we'd first arrived on set, we were told that it wasn't likely we would meet stars Chris Pine (Kirk), Zachary Quinto (Spock), and Karl Urban (Bones), because it was their day off – but here they were, in the flesh, on the set with us!

Everyone was extremely excited, and the guys were so kind and happy to see us. We spent a few minutes asking questions and getting photos before they had to take off to enjoy the rest of their day. It was, genuinely, one of the most exciting parts of *our* day, especially since none of us were expecting it. How many people can say they got to meet Kirk, Spock, and Bones in the flesh?! And still, the day was not over. We were taken to a sound stage, where we got to watch them film some incredible visual effects stunts.

Finally our on-set journey drew to a close. We were taken back out to the studio lot, where we were once again thanked generously by the producers. They told us that it was such a pleasure to have us on set, especially because it made it easy to remember why it is they go to work every day, to make this film — for the fans.

That evening we headed back to the city for a last dinner together, where we reminisced over the perfect day. We played a *Star Trek* trivia game (which I won for my team), and enjoyed an adorable cake with the Starfleet insignia iced on top. It was so much fun hanging out with everyone one last time, and we all made sure to exchange contact info so we could stay in touch. I'm Facebook friends with everyone, and we still chat every now and then. It's so cool that *Star Trek* and Omaze were able to forge friendships between people who may never otherwise have met, or thought to have spoken to each other. Omaze is an incredible organization that raises money for so many charities, and I'll never forget how amazing they made the entire experience for all of us. ⋀

Cake – the baking frontier

ONE LAST GIFT

The production had one final surprise for us before we left. Before coming to Vancouver, we'd been told that unfortunately we wouldn't be able to visit the *Enterprise* set, because it had already been struck (*dismantled – Ed.*)

Grand-prize winner Adam Horwitz celebrates with Audrianna

However, as a special thanks for visiting, the crew wanted to present each of us with a unique, framed piece of the *Enterprise* set to take home. It was amazing, and I was almost overcome with tears. I couldn't believe I'd have my very own piece of the *Enterprise*!

What was truly incredible about the visit was how welcoming and generous the entire team from Bad Robot and Paramount were. Everyone was so kind, and they went out of their way to make us comfortable. It could have been so easy to go through the motions, and get us off set as quickly as possible so we'd be out of their way, but they made sure to give us a truly remarkable experience that we would remember forever.

Being able to meet the actors I've admired for so many years was truly a highlight, but I think what I loved most was getting to speak with all of the amazing people behind the scenes, who were making this film possible. Seeing the scale of the sets, and all of the hard work that was being put into this thing for fans like me, was amazing, and I don't think I have ever loved *Star Trek* more than I did in that moment.

Anton Yelchin and Simon Pegg

ENTERPRISE
THE LEGEND LIVES ON...

Enterprise. The dictionary definition of the word is "An undertaking, especially one of some scope, complication, and risk" – a fitting description of Starfleet's most famous exploration vessel, and its mission to venture into the unknown, to discover what lies beyond the boundaries of human knowledge and understanding.

Kirk's ship was not the first to bear that name, nor will it be the last...

Words: John Ainsworth

Throughout history, there have been many ships named *Enterprise*, with one of the earliest being the 17th/18th Century French frigate *L'Enterprise*, captured by the British in 1705 and renamed the *HMS Enterprize*. Britain's Royal Navy has had 13 ships called *Enterprise* or *Enterprize*, whilst the United States Navy had eight, six of which were commissioned and therefore included the '*USS*' (United States Ship) prefix. The *USS Enterprise* aircraft carrier, CVN-65, even made a guest appearance in *Star Trek IV: The Voyage Home*, although its 'part' was actually played by another ship, the *U.S.S. Ranger*.

Following a letter campaign by *Star Trek* fans, NASA's first space shuttle was christened *Enterprise*, although it would only be used for test flights within the Earth's atmosphere, and never ventured into outer space. However, in *Star Trek*'s fictional universe, the space shuttle *Enterprise* OV-01 – a re-usable space vehicle launched in the late 20th Century employed to convey passengers and equipment to lower Earth orbit – was the first of two ships christened *Enterprise* . The *U.S.S. Enterprise* XCV 330 was a further development of the space flight program, but it was with the launch of the *Enterprise NX-01* in 2151 that Earth's journey to the stars really began.

The original *NCC-1701*

BEHIND THE SCENES

The original *Enterprise* was created by the art director and designer of the original *Star Trek* series, Matt Jefferies, who also designed the sets for the interior of the ship. Jefferies initially created a three-foot demonstration model of the ship. Once this was approved by *Star Trek* creator Gene Roddenberry, an 11-foot model was constructed by Volmer Jensen's model shop and was used in the production of the first *Star Trek* pilot, "The Cage". The model was then slightly modified for the second pilot, "Where No Man Has Gone Before", and then modified further for the series proper. Shots of all three variants are used throughout the three original series of *Star Trek*. Jefferies' distinctive design for the *Enterprise* would form the basis of all future interpretations of the vessel and, indeed, many other starships seen in the *Star Trek* TV shows and movies. Jeffies' original production model of the *Enterprise* is currently undergoing restoration, before returning to permanent display at the National Air and Space Museum, at the Smithsonian Institute in Washington DC.

The frigate

The aircraft carrier

The Space Shuttle

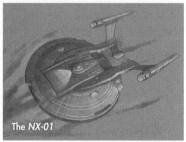
The *NX-01*

AN *ENTERPRISE* FOR
ALL TIMELINES

Following Zefram Cochrane's successful attempt to travel faster than the speed of light in 2063, work commenced over the next three decades on the development of the warp drive. This culminated in the creation of the first warp 5 engine, which would make travel between the stars, in comparatively short time spans, an achievable goal. The *Enterprise* NX-01 was the first ship to be built with the warp 5 engine and, commanded by Captain Jonathan Archer, its launch marked the beginning of mankind's exploration of interstellar space.

One of the most celebrated ships to bear the name *Enterprise* was the *U.S.S. Enterprise* NCC-1701, the first of Starfleet's NCC-17 deep space explorers. Originally commanded by Captain Christopher Pike, during the *Narada* crisis, a young firebrand named James T. Kirk, fresh out of the Academy, was awarded the captain's chair following his valiant efforts to save Earth from certain destruction at the hands of the psychopathic Romulan Nero.

Following a shakedown cruise, and a confrontation with rogue Starfleet Admiral Marcus, the *Enterprise* was tasked with a five-year mission of exploration and, captained by Kirk, she became famous for discovering many new worlds, and making first contact with over 20 new civilizations. ⋀

Zephram Cockrane's *Phoenix*

Archer's *Enterprise* NX-01

BEHIND THE SCENES

The *Enterprise*'s first movie refit

For *Star Trek: The Motion Picture*, a refitted version of the *Enterprise* was introduced. Based on Matt Jefferies' designs for the aborted *Star Trek: Phase II* TV series, Andrew Probert was responsible for the design and construction of the new *Enterprise* model. This new model would be used to represent the NCC-1701 for the first three original *Star Trek* movies.

The alternate timeline version of the NCC-1701 was a CGI model designed by Ryan Church. Although clearly based on Matt Jefferies' original version of the *Enterprise*, Church also incorporated elements introduced in the earlier *Star Trek* movies.

Narrowly avoiding total destruction in *Star Trek (2009)*, and even more narrowly in *Star Trek Into Darkness*, this version of the starship finally yielded to dramatic necessity in *Star Trek Beyond...*

STRANGE SAME WORLDS...

THE *STAR TREK* GUIDE TO MULTIVERSE THEORY

This year, 2016, marks the 50th anniversary of the original *Star Trek* television series' first screening on US television. If you're more familiar with the 21st Century's cinematic take on the show, it was the same... only different. It's almost like they happened in two different universes!

Words: Chris Dows

When J.J. Abrams brought his vision of *Star Trek* to cinema screens in 2009, many wondered how he might add a new spin to the voyages of the *U.S.S. Enterprise*. The path he chose was one that has been tried and tested many times in science fiction, and in the various *Star Trek* TV series that aired between 1966 and 2005.

The new film used Multiverse theory to create an alternate *Star Trek* reality, allowing the creative team to re-imagine the *Star Trek* universe, while retaining its familiar characters and locations. It proved fertile ground for storytelling once again in *Star Trek Into Darkness*, with guest villain Khan (from the original series episode "Space Seed," and the movie *Star Trek II: The Wrath of Khan*), and the reappearance of Leonard Nimoy's Spock, forming a bridge between the "old" and "new" timelines.

INFINITE INFINITIES

It might surprise you to learn that Multiverse theory actually exists, although it has only gained widespread acceptance as a science in recent years. In fact, the idea of differing plains of existence reaches far back into the beginnings of most world religions, so the concepts have been around for nearly as long as humans can remember.

The term "Multiverse" was first coined by the American philosopher William James, in 1895, and has been redefined throughout the 20th Century to include theories on how parallel universes and realities might come to exist. Virtually all of the arguments are based on the same starting point – that matter, even at the subatomic level, can only be combined in a finite number of ways. If these elements are mixed-up an infinite amount of times, it would mathematically result in universes that could be identical, differ in one incredibly minor way, or be totally alien to each other.

THE BIG BANG THEORY

Many supporters of Multiverse theory agree that all the combinations that can exist were created in one event – the Big Bang, the "explosion" of matter that gave birth to the universe as we know it. Some scientists go even further, suggesting that further Big Bangs – or multiple "eternal inflation" events – might still be happening.

For those who theorise a "flat" universe (most illustrations show it as a disc), there is the theory of the "quilted" Multiverse, which suggests that the membranes of one existence continuously collide with others, and reform through new Big Bangs, leading to a cyclical birth-to-death-to-rebirth pattern.

THE BLACK HOLE

How could we find – and visit – these Multiverses? One of the most popular ideas concerns black holes, which contain points of singularity that form a boundary between what we know of as the universe and the unknown. Physical laws, such as electromagnetism or gravity, might be altered within them, which could lead to a completely different kind of existence. Stars collapse in on themselves to create black holes all the time, so alternate realities could constantly be being generated, without us ever knowing.

Of all the theories, this is perhaps the easiest to grasp – far easier than the concept of "Quantum Multiverses", which are based on probabilities rather than outcomes, so every time there is a chance to make more than one choice, a new reality is created for each.

This brings us back to *Star Trek*, where at least one Multiverse was created by the choices and actions of Nero, as he pursued Spock throughout the new timeline. Perhaps he created even more! ∧

THE PRIME UNIVERSE

The timeline seen in the original *Star Trek* series, the Prime Universe was the touchstone for all events, in every version of *Star Trek* on TV and in cinemas, up until J.J. Abrams' 2009 *Star Trek* movie.

The Prime Universe timeline does not cease to exist, despite the actions of Nero, and aspects of it will continue to be explored in the new *Star Trek* television series, set to hit screens in 2017.

THE ALTERNATE UNIVERSE

The Alternate Universe begins with Nero's destruction of the *U.S.S. Kelvin*. From that point on, things inexorably change – particularly for the young James T. Kirk, whose early Starfleet career is quite different to that of the Kirk in the Prime Universe timeline.

More significant changes come with the destruction of Vulcan, and then the attack on Section 31's London base by Khan Noonien Singh in *Into Darkness*. *Star Trek Beyond* promises to continue this blend of the familiar and the new.

THE MIRROR UNIVERSE

Perhaps the best known of *Star Trek*'s Multiverses, the Mirror Universe is a place of sinister parallel versions of the characters we know and love, as seen in the original series episode "Mirror, Mirror," in which the Prime Universe Captain Kirk met evil versions of his entire crew, and vice versa!

Deep Space Nine made several visits to the Mirror Universe, with Captain Sisko having to deal with twisted versions of Kira Nerys, Miles O'Brien, and even his own deceased wife. Even prequel series *Star Trek: Enterprise* got in on the act, in the episode "In a Mirror, Darkly."

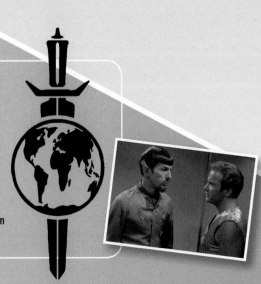

KARL URBAN

BONES

From Middle Earth to Mega City One, Karl Urban is no stranger to the worlds of science fiction and fantasy. In *Star Trek Beyond*, he's back as wry medic Leonard "Bones" McCoy, and enjoying life on the final frontier.

Words: Bryan Cairns

Star Trek Magazine: **When this project was coming together, there must have been plenty of curiosity and anticipation regarding the new script. What excited you about it when it finally arrived?**
Karl Urban: I was thrilled when I first read it. Simon Pegg and Doug Jung did a fantastic job of delivering an action-packed, character-driven script. The thing I responded to most was the development of the relationships between the characters. It's not forced. It's earned. I was probably most thrilled with my scenes in the film opposite Spock, who I spend quite a lot of the movie with. That's a great pairing.

STM: **You championed the idea for the** *Enterprise* **to begin its five-year mission in the movie. Why was that important to you?**
KU: It was important to me because that's

what I originally fell in love with when I was a kid, watching the original series and that five-year mission. It just seems like a natural evolution to take this reboot. Obviously, there's an entire galaxy of stories and characters, and possibilities.

STM: **Part of** *Star Trek*'s **appeal is discovering those new planets and civilizations...**
KU: Absolutely, and that's certainly the case in this film. For a great period of the film, we're on an extraordinary planet. It was amazing to shoot those sequences. The planet itself is an interesting character.

STM: **How pleased were you to get off the ship again?**
KU: I enjoy being on the bridge of the *Enterprise*. In this film, it's grander in scale. I was very excited I got to "beam" in this film, which I didn't get to do in the previous two.

STM: *Star Trek Beyond* **pairs up a lot of the crewmembers. How do Bones and Spock bounce off each other?**
KU: It's as you would expect. The wonderful thing about pairing those two together is they are diametrically opposed to each other in

"THAT'S THE CHALLENGE OF THESE NEW MOVIES. IT'S NOT ONLY TO BE RESPECTFUL TO WHAT HAS COME IN THE PAST, BUT ALSO TO EXPLORE NEW TERRITORY."

Preparing for some
Star Trek Beyond action

their perspectives – cultural, historical, and as beings. Their relationship is taken to a new level – a level I don't believe we've seen before in *Star Trek*. To me, I think that's the challenge of these new movies. It's not only to be respectful of what has come in the past, but also to explore new territory. That's what this film does remarkably well.

STM: Viewers have been waiting for more Bones/Spock/Kirk. How will that iconic trinity develop more?

KU: What I love about *Star Trek Beyond* is you get to see elements of the relationships that are traditional. For example, you get to see Bones be a conciliary to Kirk, and a dear friend to Kirk. In *Into Darkness*, that relationship somewhat felt inferred. It's nice to have that really affirmed in this film. And, as I previously said, the relationship with Spock develops wonderfully. There's a deeper understanding between the two characters as a result of their experience.

STM: What makes Krall such a formidable foe?
KU: He's a worthy adversary because, like all good villains, he forces the protagonists to question themselves and to question their direction. A good villain defines the morality of the heroes, and that's certainly the case in *Star Trek Beyond*.

STM: Some of *Enterprise's* crewmembers experience "cabin fever" during this five-year mission, and begin to question their place and purpose. How does the film challenge *Star Trek*'s core values, and how happy were you with the answers?
KU: *Star Trek* has always fundamentally been about family. This film challenges the crew, because that family is broken up. Each of us, in our different ways, is faced with a choice and a set of challenges. Ultimately, I feel at the end of

this story that this crew bonded together in a real and valid experience-driven manner. That connection takes time to buy. In this film, you really feel that family is earned.

Star Trek Beyond also builds on the relationships established in the first two films. It explores new territory. It takes these characters to new places. As a result of the experience they all go through in this film, they're a lot closer. The script that Simon and Doug have written – after the first two films – you come to a far deeper understanding of all the characters in this. It's so rewarding.

STM: Bones famously spouts memorable one-liners. What do you love about his dialogue?

"I WAS VERY EXCITED I GOT TO 'BEAM' IN THIS FILM, WHICH I DIDN'T GET TO DO IN THE PREVIOUS TWO."

KU: It's his point of view that I love, and his expression of character. I've been pretty blessed with some fantastic dialogue, particularly from the first film. I had such amazing lines as, "Space is full of disease and danger, wrapped in darkness and silence." In *Star Trek Beyond*, I had a fantastic time collaborating with Doug and Simon to deliver what we believe to be some truly quintessential Bones beats. We also have a lot more fun in this film with the traditional tropes.

STM: Justin Lin took over directing duties from J.J. Abrams for *Star Trek Beyond*. How were those initial meetings and discussions?
KU: It was actually talking to Justin that convinced me to do the movie. It became clear McCoy was going to have a valid function in this film. That's something I had been yearning for, to actually see the depth and meaning of his friendship with Kirk, and to further develop and cement his role. There was a lot more for McCoy to do in this picture. After talking to Justin, I signed on.

STM: Another of your noteworthy sci-fi roles is *Dredd*. How would you compare the *Dredd* and *Star Trek* universes?

> "IT'S AN HONOR AND A PRIVILEGE TO BE PART OF SOMETHING THAT REPRESENTS A VISION OF MANKIND FUNCTIONING AT ITS BEST."

KU: They are quite different. *Dredd* is a much bleaker vision of the future. The *Star Trek* universe is a vision of humanity that is full of hope and optimism. Mankind has moved past committing genocide upon each other, and has united, and is now exploring space. That's part of *Star Trek*'s enduring appeal.

STM: What are your thoughts on more Bones and *Star Trek*?

KU: At this point, I'm just focused on *Star Trek Beyond*. We're at that point where we're handing over something we've labored over – and loved dearly – to its audience. If the audience embraces it and loves it as much as we did making it, it would be a privilege to come back and make another one.

STM: As a fan of science fiction, what has it meant to you to be part of the *Star Trek* legacy, and to celebrate its 50th anniversary this year?
KU: I feel it's an honor and a privilege to be part of something that represents a vision of mankind functioning at its best. *Star Trek* has brought a lot of people a lot of joy and entertainment over the 50 years. It's unique in its qualities. It was originally sexy and action-packed and thought-provoking. At its best, it helps us focus on the best aspects that we can aspire to achieve in our direction as a race.

I have gotten a fantastic group of friends out of it. To me, that's the most important thing. This cast is phenomenal. We enjoy each other's company. They are an absolute pleasure to work with. ▲

ENTERPRISE NCC-1701
CREW MANIFEST

LEONARD H. McCOY

Rank: Lieutenant Commander
Position: Chief Medical Officer; Ship's Doctor
Species: Human
Date of Birth: 2227
Place of Birth: Georgia, USA, Earth

Already a practising doctor, McCoy joined Starfleet following a painful divorce that left him with nothing but his "bones" to his name (hence the nickname that Jim Kirk gave him).

Irascible yet big-hearted, McCoy is a highly ethical and moral physician of the highest caliber, and loyal to a fault. His closest personal friendship is with Kirk, although those closest to him would note that his relationship with Spock – abrasive though it might appear – is equally important.

McCoy initiated Starfleet Academy's first Astrophobia seminar, because of his own fear of space... and technology, and transporters, and confined space, and aliens...

McCOY'S FINEST MOMENTS

Despite McCoy's nervousness about space travel, and the dangers it entails, the quick-witted medic isn't afraid to take risks when it means saving lives...

- McCoy risked his career to smuggle Kirk onboard the *Enterprise*, creating a fake medical emergency to sneak him past security even though Kirk was technically grounded.
- When Doctor Puri was killed during the *Enterprise*'s first battle with the *Narada*, McCoy immediately stepped in as the ship's Chief Medical Officer (*Star Trek* (2009)).
- No stranger to visiting alien worlds, McCoy's risk-averse nature is often offset by Kirk's knack for adventure, as when he and Kirk were chased by a local tribe of Nibirans over the edge of a cliff!
- McCoy displayed his medical genius when he uncovered the nature of Khan's genetic engineering by testing its regenerative properties on a dead Tribble, which would ultimately allow McCoy to use Khan's blood to save Kirk's life (*Star Trek Into Darkness*).

"I DON'T NEED A DOCTOR, DAMN IT! I AM A DOCTOR!"

JOHN CHO

SULU

John Cho's brave, resourceful, and ever-calm Hikaru Sulu is a safe pair of hands at the controls of the Starship *Enterprise* – but the five-year mission has left its mark on the man.

Is Sulu's destiny a captain's chair of his own, or a return to his family, light years away on planet Earth?

Words: Bryan Cairns

Star Trek Magazine: As the movie hits cinemas, many of *Star Trek Beyond*'s plot details have remained successfully under wraps. How secretive was the process of getting the script, reading it, and then actually filming?
John Cho: I guess I'm accustomed to it now, but it's pretty secretive. It seemed like we were under a little less scrutiny [this time], because we were shooting out of the country [in Vancouver, Canada]. The script is printed on red paper, so it's not photocopy-able, there are watermarks on every page, the sides (*pages of the script – Ed.*) are collected at the end of the

day. To be honest, it's a pain. I understand why we go through it. There is an actual reason for it, and it's not just protecting the studio's property. From J.J. Abrams, at least, I always understood it as protecting the experience of the moviegoer.

STM: It's been a few years since *Star Trek Into Darkness* hit the big screen. How did it feel, that first day back on set, slipping into Sulu's uniform again, and reuniting with the gang?
JC: This one was a blend of new and old. There was a sense of familiarity, because we were together with the main cast. There was a new director. There were some tweaks to the look – the *Enterprise* has been tweaked a little bit, but not much, the uniforms were different, as Michael Kaplan did not design the wardrobe for this one.

There was some optimism, there were some nerves, but generally it felt familiar, because the crew was the crew. We've spent a lot of time together over the years.

STM: This installment features some huge personal developments for Sulu. How surprised were you to learn the movie would be exploring his fatherhood?
JC: Sulu has a daughter in the alternate timeline, and I didn't know it was going

John Cho as Hikaru Sulu, in *Star Trek (2009)*

"THERE ARE A LOT OF PARALLELS BETWEEN BEING A PART OF THE CREW OF THE STARSHIP *ENTERPRISE* AND BEING AN ACTOR."

Sulu (John Cho) and the crew prepare for trouble in *Star Trek Beyond*

Helmsman Hikaru Sulu

to come up in this one. I was excited about it, in terms of giving him some personal space. What we shot, and what I read, puts some personal stakes to the larger mission.

STM: One of the film's big themes tackles what it's like being on a long-term, deep space mission. In what ways does this undertaking affect Sulu?

JC: For him, in this instance, it's being away from loved ones for a long time, which is easy to relate to for me. There are a lot of parallels between being a part of the crew of the Starship *Enterprise* and being an actor. There's going away from home on these projects, and becoming very intimate with this group of co-workers, and sacrificing for one another, becoming very intimate with them for a sustained period of time. Hopefully, that's the ideal cast – people who sacrifice for one another, and give to one another. Then you're off to do your family thing.

It's a tough thing to juggle. It can feel weird sometimes. When you're shooting, it's the most important thing in your life for that period of time. That's primarily what I felt in this installment for Sulu. For other crewmembers, I think there's a sense of, "Are we actually getting something done out here, or, are we just spinning our wheels?"

STM: It seems like the *Enterprise* team splits into pairs in this movie. Kirk and Chekov. Spock and Bones. Who does Sulu spend more time with, and what was fun about that dynamic?

JC: Uhura is the answer. For John Cho, that means spending a lot of time with Zoe Saldana, which is great. She's an amazing glass of lemonade. Zoe has a very bright, light energy.

You have these group scenes, and everyone is chipping in here and there. Sometimes it's nice to get a two-person [scene] and focus your energy on one other person. I got to do that with Zoe. It's pleasurable, and easy, to look into her eyes and believe.

"TO SOME EXTENT, THE QUAGMIRE THAT SULU FINDS HIMSELF IN AT THE BEGINNING OF THE MOVIE IS DUE TO HIS AMBITION."

John Cho as Sulu

STM: There hasn't been much interaction previously between Sulu and Uhura. Was it good to mix things up?
JC: Doug Jung was telling me that he and Simon Pegg had wondered if we had ever spoken to each other in the first two films. They went back and realized we hadn't. They really liked the idea of pairing us up, but I just realized they were wrong – in *Into Darkness* we had a scene together.

STM: *Star Trek Beyond* features a new big bad. What makes Krall such a foe to be reckoned with?
JC: It's hard to say. He's played by Idris Elba, who's very formidable, and a pleasure to work with and watch. He's really good, and enormous. The composite [character design] I saw was

incredibly frightening. Krall is passionate about what he wants to achieve, and bloodthirsty when it comes to eliminating anything that stands in his way. He's an interesting bad guy.

STM: Elba is almost unrecognizable in all that make-up, too.
JC: One of the things I find interesting about Idris is how he stands. I'm a connoisseur of stances. I would recognize him even if I didn't know the actor. Coming into it, I would have thought, "That guy stands like Idris."

> "IT'S BEEN A REAL HONOR TO HAVE AN ASSOCIATION WITH SOMETHING THAT PREDATES ME, AND WILL OUTLIVE ME."

STM: Does that make you even more self-aware of your own posture?
JC: Sadly, I am unable to change my stance. I think about it sometimes, like "I've got to stand like that guy," or, "That's good, or interesting." I would recognize each of our crewmembers in silhouette. Obviously, Zoe has a very different silhouette, but I would recognize each of our crewmembers from their torso alignment.

STM: *Star Trek Beyond* marks the first new *Star Trek* movie without J.J. Abrams behind the camera. What impressed you about director Justin Lin, and the way he approached the material?
JC: Justin came from a place of respect – attention to detail, and respect for the actors. I just like his process. He's like Columbo (the 1970s TV detective). He puts his hands behind his back, and walks around a problem until an answer appears. He's kind of relentless.

It was mostly the totality of his involvement. He's so into what the visual effects are going to be, and the world that he's creating. At the same time, he obsesses over the arrangement of

ENTERPRISE NCC-1701 CREW MANIFEST

HIKARU SULU

Rank: Lieutenant
Position: Helm
Species: Human
Date of Birth: 2237
Place of Birth: San Francisco, USA, Earth
Hikaru Sulu is focused, decisive, and an ace pilot, with a strong sense of humor and irony. As the *Enterprise* helmsman, he has proven his aptitude for command under pressure on numerous occasions.

Top of his Starfleet graduating class in Astro-Sciences and Advanced Botany, Sulu founded Starfleet Academy's European Swordsmanship Club. He is also a family man, and keeps a picture of his daughter on his command station on the *Enterprise* Bridge. Sulu struggles to resolve the conflict he feels between following his career and nurturing his family.

SULU'S FINEST MOMENTS
Sulu's coolness under pressure, skills as a pilot, and sense of duty have saved the *Enterprise* and its crew many times...
- In a bid to stop the vengeful Nero's attack on Vulcan, Sulu (alongside Kirk and Chief Engineer Olson) performed a dangerous space-dive onto the Romulan drilling rig. Engaging in life-threatening hand-to-hand combat – using a retractable sword to fence against the more heavily armed Romulans – Sulu's skills saved Kirk's life.
- To hide the *Enterprise* from Nero's ship, the *Narada*, Sulu piloted the Starfleet flagship deep into the perilous rings of Saturn. There, the planet's turbulent magnetic forces would interfere with the Romulan mining ship's sensors (*Star Trek* (2009)).
- In an effort to save the Nibiru race from extinction, Sulu piloted a shuttle inside an active volcano to enable Spock to activate a cold-fusion device to stop it erupting.

- Sulu took command of the *Enterprise* while Kirk and Spock went after John Harrison (AKA Khan Noonien Singh). He would later refuse to leave his post and abandon ship as the damaged *Enterprise* plummeted towards Earth (*Star Trek Into Darkness*).
Words: Rich Matthews

"'CAPTAIN' DOES HAVE A NICE RING TO IT."

Cho gets direction from J.J.Abrams on the set of *Star Trek (2009)*

words in a line, or the eyeline to an explosion. He gets very obsessed over each and every detail. From our point of view, we felt we were being really taken care of, which is all you can ask for from a director.

STM: **The film's trailer was jam-packed with explosions and fight sequences. How much action does Sulu get to see?**
JC: There's not a lot for me. What I will say is it wasn't so much physically challenging as it was, "Oh, I see..." Justin has a very unique understanding of movement. It's been interesting for me to watch. Even what you read as a very simple scene, where there's no indication of anybody moving, he knows how to subtly move a camera, or block something so there's always story being told by movement. It's not something I became aware of until halfway through. Looking back, that's something I came away feeling impressed by.

STM: **Sulu has always been very competent, and audiences loved seeing him get in on the action in the 2009 *Star Trek* movie. How has he moved forward over three films?**
JC: That's a tough one to answer. I hope he's relaxing a little bit, becoming a little more human, and showing some of his ambition, which I feel is a darker quality. To some extent, the quagmire that Sulu finds himself in at the beginning of the movie is due to his ambition. He's always been goal-oriented, but there's

a dark side to that too. He has to deal with it a little bit in this one.

STM: **What do you enjoy about being involved in these larger-than-life blockbusters?**
JC: Acting is acting. Having a good cast is a good cast. A good script is a good script. With *Star Trek* in particular, there's an extra tickle. For me, it's being part of something that I consider to be a very important part of pop culture, and popular American culture. That's something interesting, and it allows me to connect with different kinds of people, and meet different kinds of people. There's an extra pleasure in that.

STM: **What are your thoughts on doing more *Star Trek*? How hard would it be saying goodbye to this cast, character, and universe?**
JC: It would make me sad, I guess. If it is goodbye, I say thank you, because it's changed

my life for the better. As I said, it's been a real honor to have an association with something that predates me, and will outlive me. That's unusual. For whatever reason, and I have my ideas, it seems to be important to a lot of people. It keeps finding a place in the hearts of generations of Americans... or Earthlings, I should say. I just feel honored to be connected to that. That doesn't come along very often, and I'm aware of that.

JAYLAH

With her distinctive monochrome make-up and kick-ass moves, Sofia Boutella's turn as mysterious alien Jaylah in *Star Trek Beyond* looks set to ruffle more than Kirk's feathers.

Words: Christopher Cooper

Star Trek Magazine: Your character, Jaylah, is new to the *Star Trek* universe. Can you tell us a little bit about where she's from, and what role she plays in the movie?

Sofia Boutella: She's sort of a feisty survivor. A loner who has been on her own for quite a while, and learned to survive on her own. She has a lot of personality and, very much like Captain Kirk, she has her own way of doing things. She's a bit stubborn, she's mouthy, but lovely at the same time, and has an energy about her, "I know what I'm doing, and I'll do it myself!"

STM: The make-up that you wear in the film is very striking. Did it help you find the character?

SB: Oh, completely. At first, when I had the make-up put on me, I thought "what remarkable work." I've never seen anything like it. And they're very good at what they do; [make-up designer] Joel Harlow is a magician, really. And the more I had the prosthetic on, it was harder to imagine Jaylah *without* it on. There's weight to it, even if it wasn't that much, and the ponytail has a certain weight. There was a certain feel to it. It's like when you wear a pair of heels between wearing your sneakers – you feel different. It will be intense; you will be in the character immediately. It would be difficult to play Jaylah without all that going on.

STM: The prosthetics are subtle. With the white and black make-up, it's difficult to say where the prosthetics end and you begin.

SB: It's very subtle, but because it's subtle work, it took a long time [to apply]. I think four hours. It's on my nose and then the forehead a bit, but the bottom part of my face is me, entirely me. Then I had contacts, and those black lines are actually prosthetic. They are raised.

STM: Had you done any prosthetics work before?

SB: No, never. It was the first time.

STM: Jaylah is a very physical role, she does a lot of fighting. You trained as a dancer from a very early age, and you were a gymnast as well. How much was your experience as a physical artist of benefit in playing her?

SB: Entirely. It was very helpful to use my dancing ability, and what I've learned as a dancer, to execute everything that was required of me. I definitely used some of my old tricks, my body language, or treating things as a choreography, or looking at things with a rhythm so I could learn them. It's definitely helpful to have a dance background to do all this fight training.

STM: And because you play an alien character, were you able to call upon that physicality to give Jaylah an alien feel?

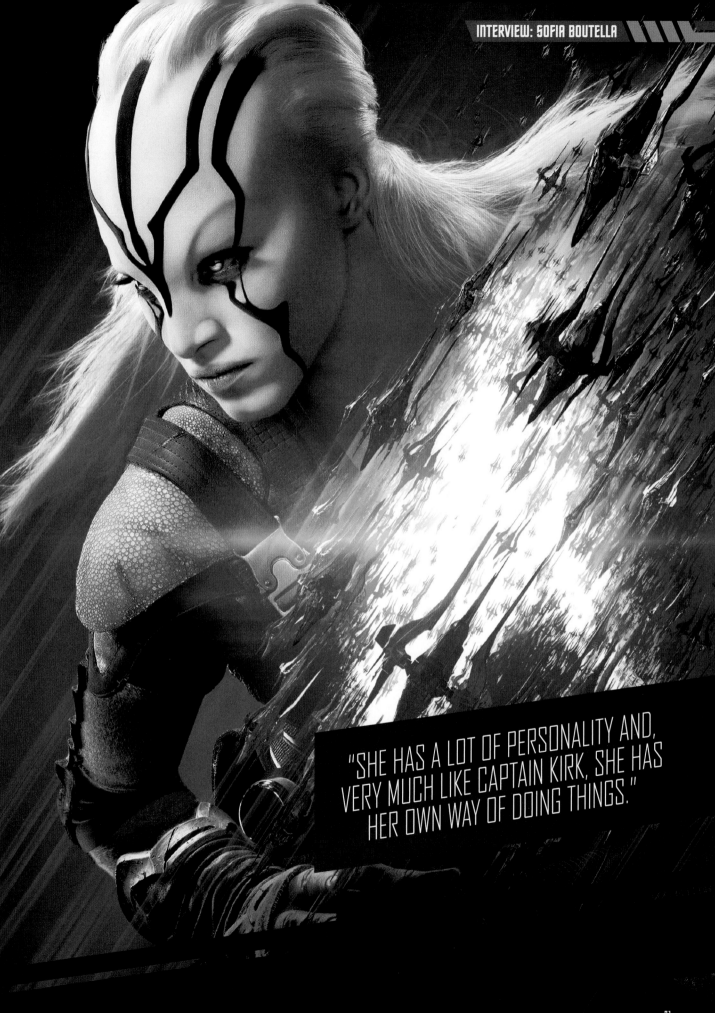

"SHE HAS A LOT OF PERSONALITY AND, VERY MUCH LIKE CAPTAIN KIRK, SHE HAS HER OWN WAY OF DOING THINGS."

SB: Yes, it is helpful to have that sort of body consciousness. I think you really need to find how your character moves, how she sits, how she walks, all that sort of thing is very important. I definitely use it.

STM: I assume that you did quite a few of your own fight scene stunts, as you did in *Kingsman*? Did you have to pick up any new skills for *Star Trek*?
SB: I trained in parkour, or "free running." I did that, and then I did bo-staff, which is a traditional martial arts discipline with a long bamboo stick, so I trained in those two disciplines, specifically for Jaylah.

STM: It takes some nerve, even for a former gymnast, to take up parkour.

Boutella spent four hours in the make-up chair to become Jaylah

SB: It was a lot of fun to learn, to be honest, though at first I said, "I'm never going to be able to do this," because it's quite hard. And then you're taught, and then you learn. You practise, and then you learn.

STM: Simon Pegg has said that, as he was writing Jaylah, he gave her a unique speech pattern. You're originally from Algeria, and you moved to France when you were young. Did that diversity help you with the way she speaks?
SB: I definitely tried *not* to speak with my French accent. It would be weird for an alien, wouldn't it? Finding [her] language and speech pattern, it was very interesting to discover. Because Jaylah's character has never existed before, everything needed to be done. Discovering that was fun to play around with.

STM: How familiar were you with Star Trek before you were cast?
SB: I didn't grow up with it. I wasn't a Trekkie. I knew what it was, but my family didn't watch it, and I didn't watch it either. Not because I didn't like it or anything, it just wasn't something we watched. But certainly, I watched the first films of the new franchise, and when I got the role I did my research, and watched the TV shows and the old franchise, all of them.

STM: Was there any aspect of those old Star Treks that made you think, "yeah, I get this"?
SB: I really like the message it conveys. I really like the message about people being diverse, and different, and within that diversity, unity takes place, and embracing one another within those differences. This is something that I really liked.

STM: You've joined an established cast, who've worked together previously and are very close. How did you find working with them, and becoming a part of that?
SB: It's always tricky to join a family that's been tied [together] for such a long time. I wasn't terrified or anything, I just thought, "I hope it's going to work out, and that I'm going to belong to them," you know? And then they dearly welcomed me with open arms, and made me a part of the family quite quickly, which made it

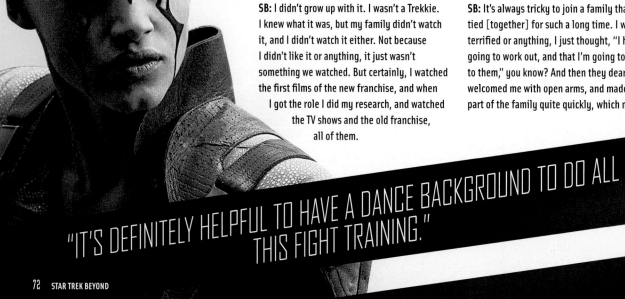

"IT'S DEFINITELY HELPFUL TO HAVE A DANCE BACKGROUND TO DO ALL THIS FIGHT TRAINING."

very helpful and easy for me. They were all very lovely to me, and it's very much like family. We get together, and we're very tight.

STM: Many of your scenes are with Kirk, and you spend time with Scotty as well. How was that experience? Did you enjoy filming those scenes?
SB: I loved it. They're amazing human beings, and they're so good at what they do. It was also great to observe Simon. It was funny, because he would be on set, acting, and then all of a sudden he would run to his chair and grab his laptop.

Director Justin Lin talks Boutella through a scene (*Star Trek Beyond*)

I was saying, "What are you doing?", and he's like, "I'm writing the script," and then he'd run back, "Right, got to be on set, I'm now an actor," and then, no, wait, he's going back to writing.

STM: Looking back over your career, it strikes me that you've moved forward somewhat organically, from one experience to the next. Did you ever have a game-plan, or do you prefer to accept opportunities when they seem interesting?

> "I REALLY LIKE THE MESSAGE ABOUT PEOPLE BEING DIVERSE, AND DIFFERENT, AND WITHIN THAT DIVERSITY, UNITY TAKES PLACE."

SB: My first job ever, when I was 17, was an acting job. My friend told me "There's this audition for this movie, and they're looking for dancers. Do you want to come?" I said yes. It was playing the love interest in a dance movie called *Dance Challenge*. I've danced since I was five, so I booked that film and, from the age of 17 to 19, I did movies in France. Small movies that you probably wouldn't know of. Then I stopped acting when I was 19, because I really just wanted to dance.

STM: After which, you toured as a dancer with the likes of Madonna. What was it that prompted that decision?
SB: I felt like I was a bit all over the place, and then I did not act from 19 to 24. I moved to Los Angeles, just because I had two more months on my visa after my first tour with Madonna. I thought I was just going to stay a little bit, and ended up staying for ten years. All that time I kept taking classes, and learned by doing theater.

STM: So when did you reach the decision to stop dancing and concentrate on acting?
SB: At the age of 27, I asked myself, "Okay, what do you want to do, acting or dancing?" and I couldn't pick. I couldn't possibly bring myself to think about not dancing anymore. Eventually, I just woke up one day and thought, "My heart is with acting." Dancing will always be part of me, and I always use

it, but it's just not what I wanted to do anymore. And then I didn't work for three years! I didn't make a pay check in two years. It was quite tough. I auditioned for all sorts of movies, I didn't just do Hollywood stuff. Actually *Star Trek* is the first Hollywood project I've acted in.

STM: But now those three years of hardship seem to be paying off. You're currently shooting Universal's *The Mummy*, playing the Mummy, so what's next?
SB: I was very lucky to [be cast in] *Kingsman*, and the exposure has helped me. I'm not opposed to physical roles, as long as there's a story in there, or some potential behind it that's meaningful, but that's not all I'm looking for in a project.

I'm very green to this world, I'm still learning a lot, so I just consider everything a learning experience. Just taking on a character is fun for me. Anything you give me, I can have fun with, to be honest. The more characters I play, the more I'll be able to define what I want to do, but right now, I'd be up for anything. You give me a character; I'll take the challenge. Why not, you know?

STM: Wherever you go from here, part of you now belongs to *Star Trek*. How do you feel about joining that universe?
SB: It's a lot of fun. I'm very lucky to be a part of this franchise and, on top of that, to have made good friends. *Star Trek* is a clever show, and very well done. I'm very lucky to be a part of it. I love it. ▲

SOFIA BOUTELLA

Algerian-born Sofia Boutella is an actress, dancer, and musician. Moving to France in 1992, she trained as a ballet dancer, and has since danced alongside Madonna and Rihanna. More recently, her focus has switched to acting, with a starring role coming up in Universal Pictures' remake of classic monster movie, *The Mummy*.

- Eva – *StreetDance 2* (2012)
- Ara – *Monsters: Dark Continent* (2014)
- Gazelle – *Kingsman: The Secret Service* (2014)
- Shadha – *Tiger Raid* (2016)

SIMON PEGG

MONTGOMERY SCOTT

As Scotty, the *Enterprise*'s dedicated Chief Engineer, actor Simon Pegg only had the stability of the ship's warp core to worry about – that, and some complicated technical dialogue. Now, as co-writer of the latest *Star Trek* movie, *Star Trek Beyond*, he has the future of a multi-million dollar film franchise resting on his shoulders. Can his dilithium crystals handle the pressure?

Words: Christopher Cooper

Star Trek Magazine: **From the perspective of playing and writing for Scotty, how did you find the transition from being a performer in *Star Trek* to writing an entire movie screenplay?**

Simon Pegg: It was interesting. I found that I tended to be the one writing Scotty's dialogue, just because I know the character very well. I have Scottish family, so when the scripts for *Star Trek (2009)* and *Into Darkness* came in, I'd be the one saying, "No, it's the Welsh that say 'boyo,'" you know?

I felt kind of weird, because I thought, 'It's going to be strange writing Scotty, and putting him in it a lot, because I didn't want it to seem like I was writing myself a role. So I deferred to Doug [Jung, Pegg's co-writer] in terms of how much Scotty should be in it, or what his role should be, a lot of the time.

Doug would also say, "You write this scene," or "You write that scene." We never said,

'Let's have him here, and him there." Luckily, it happened very organically, and the story dictated the whereabouts of each character, and what they had to contribute.

STM: Did you have to be quite strict with yourself, not giving Scotty the best lines?

SP: I felt like I would be doing the script a disservice if I hijacked the best lines. Obviously, Doug and I wanted all the characters to have interesting dialogue. I love writing for Spock. It's really fun to write in "Spockese." We had long conversations about syntax and sentence structure, and abbreviation, and whether or not he'd use certain words. That stuff was really fun and challenging. Bones is really fun to write for, just because he's so straight-talking, he uses a lot of metaphors, and his "Southern charm" is loads of fun. Just getting the rhythms of what they say.

It was really nice to come to the table with the *dramatis personae* that we knew really well. We knew these characters. They were living, breathing, 50-year-old things. It was such a help to us, as writers, to have these fully formed, three-dimensional people to write for.

STM: Has Scotty changed much over the course of these three films?

Jaylah (Sofia Boutella) has something to show Scotty (Simon Pegg)

"I FELT LIKE I WOULD BE DOING THE SCRIPT A DISSERVICE IF I HIJACKED THE BEST LINES."

Simon Pegg as Scotty demonstrates his engineering skills, in *Star Trek Beyond*

SP: Scotty has probably changed the least, because he's been in his element, he's been in the engine room, tweaking the *Enterprise*. Scotty's as pragmatic and cantankerous as ever, but he secretly loves the opportunity to test the ship, and be present at this point in its evolution. His inter-personal dynamics with everybody have evolved. The friendships that they've forged, the relationships that they have, have moved on. They're not new to each other now. I don't think Scotty's ever felt uncomfortable speaking his mind. He's always felt that he's had Kirk's ear, because he knows and trusts him, and that Kirk trusts him back. It's been fun to play that dichotomy between a professional and personal relationship.

Keenser (Deep Roy) is back to keep Scotty company

STM: Do you feel a sense of ownership of the character now? You've played him for twice as long as James Doohan did in the original series.
SP: I do feel I know him, certainly, and I love playing him. He's a great character to play, and it's been really nice to be given the chance to put my own spin on that. I always defer to James Doohan, just because he was there first. I've inherited this character from him, and it's always been important to me that I'm aware of that. For all of us, I think, that's important. But yeah, I do feel less of a guest actor in that part now, and more that it's mine, at the moment.

STM: Would you like to play Scotty again?
SP: I'd love to, if only because the experience of making these films is so much fun. We have a blast, and the relationship between all the cast that's built up over the years is really strong, and we're very close. We enjoy the chance to hang out with each other for periods of time, and that feeds into a great affection for the stories and material, so yeah, I'd love to. It would be great. I'd love to carry on and be as old and overweight as everyone else was.

"WE HAVE A BLAST, AND THE RELATIONSHIP BETWEEN ALL THE CAST THAT'S BUILT UP OVER THE YEARS IS REALLY STRONG."

STM: As well as hooking up with Kirk in *Star Trek Beyond*, Scotty also spends time with Sofia Boutella's new character, Jaylah. You play with group dynamics a lot in this movie.

SP: There's a point of separation in the film, and everybody finds themselves in different locations. Scotty, for some period, meets up with Sofia's character, and without giving too much away, there's the gradual reuniting of everybody. That happens at different points, and in different groups. Chekov and Kirk are together for quite a while, and we liked the idea of the youngest and seemingly most naïve character pairing up with the slightly older statesman of the crew. We chose the pairings carefully, in terms of what we'd seen before, and what we thought would be interesting in terms of their personal dynamics. Scotty's on his own for a little bit, but then finds Jaylah on the way.

In this one, we wanted to create a story that was very much an ensemble, about the crew, rather than being particularly Kirk/Spock-driven, like the previous two movies had been. They were very much about their relationship, and Doug and I felt that it was time to give everybody [their chance]. Obviously Kirk and

Spock are still there, center-stage, but we didn't really hear that much from Bones in the last film, and he's such an interesting character. We wanted to divvy up screen time almost equally between everybody.

STM: You've performed in movies you written, more than most actors. How different did it feel, fulfilling both roles on a movie of this scale?

SP: I was worried, at first. I was worried that

> ## "SCOTTY'S AS PRAGMATIC AND CANTANKEROUS AS EVER, BUT HE SECRETLY LOVES THE OPPORTUNITY TO TEST THE SHIP, AND BE PRESENT AT THIS POINT IN ITS EVOLUTION."

it might change the dynamic among the cast, because we've all known each other for nearly ten years now, and there's a very familial relationship between us. We all spend time with each other when we're not on set, particularly this time, when we were up in Vancouver. But in actual fact, it kind of felt good. The cast felt quite supported, having one of their own on the other side of the camera. What I worried about actually became a bonus in the end.

We worked with each of the castmembers individually. Doug and I sent an email out, early on, saying, "Look, you know your characters, and you have ideas about them. Don't feel like you can't come and talk to us about it." So we worked with each actor to bring out not just the best in their characters, but in their performances, and that was good.

In terms of the writing, I think if I'd had time to stop and think about it, I would have just collapsed in terror. The films I've written, I've never written a film which has a budget bigger than $35 million, and this is like $200 million! It's kind of scary. ⋀

ENTERPRISE NCC-1701
CREW MANIFEST

MONTGOMERY SCOTT

Rank: Lieutenant Commander
Position: Chief Engineer
Species: Human

Date of Birth: 2222
Place of Birth: Scotland, United Kingdom, Earth

Montgomery "Scotty" Scott is headstrong and often outspoken, a rebellious miracle worker and engineering genius who truly loves what he thinks of as *his* ship, the *Enterprise*.

Scotty's obsession with engineering ensured he came first in his class on Admiral Archer's *Advanced Relativistic Mechanics* course at Starfleet Academy. Later, as an Academy aide on the course, he would also be disciplined for using Admiral Archer's prized pet beagle, Porthos, in a transwarp transporter experiment. Consequently, he was stationed on the back-of-beyond ice planet Delta Vega, where he would first meet Jim Kirk.

SCOTTY'S FINEST MOMENTS

The heroic *Enterprise* chief engineer has never been shy of expressing his views, or going beyond the line of duty to work miracles...

- With a little help from an older Spock (from the "Prime" universe, as we know it), Scotty beamed himself and Kirk off of the ice planet Delta Vega – and onto the in-warp *Enterprise*!
- Scotty ejected and then detonated the *Enterprise*'s warp core, in order to create a shock wave that would propel the ship to safety – beyond the event horizon of a black hole, created by the detonation of red matter on "Prime" Spock's ship (*Star Trek* (2009))
- When he felt his orders – to load mysterious, unscannable torpedoes onto the ship, to be used to kill John Harrison without trial – were questionable, Scotty stood up to Captain Kirk and resigned his Starfleet commission, giving up his place on the *Enterprise*.

- In an effort to stop Admiral Marcus' plan to start a war between the Federation and the Klingons – and kill everyone aboard the *Enterprise* – Scotty went "behind enemy lines" to infiltrate the top-secret *U.S.S. Vengeance* (*Star Trek Into Darkness*).

> "THE NOTION OF TRANSWARP BEAMING IS LIKE TRYING TO HIT A BULLET WITH A SMALLER BULLET, WHILST WEARING A BLINDFOLD, RIDING A HORSE."

MAKING STAR TREK BEYOND:
THE PRINCE OF PROSTHETICS
JOEL HARLOW: MAKE-UP

Having won an Oscar for his work on J.J. Abrams' first foray into the *Star Trek* universe, Joel Harlow returned to design the make-up and prosthetics for Justin Lin's *Star Trek Beyond* – with the challenge of creating over 50 brand new alien races to commemorate *Star Trek*'s 50th anniversary...

Words: Bryan Cairns

The complex make-up for Jaylah (Sophia Boutella) looks deceptively simple

Make-up designer Joel Harlow is in high demand – and for good reason. His extensive body of work includes *Pirates of the Caribbean: Curse of the Black Pearl*, *Constantine*, *The Ring Two*, *Angels & Demons*, *Dark Shadows*, *Green Lantern* and the *Buffy the Vampire Slayer* TV series. Furthermore, he's the founder of the effects studio Morphology FX. In retrospect, Harlow credits watching the original *King Kong* with his father for igniting his passion in make-up.

"I knew then that I wanted to create characters," says Harlow, taking time out from his busy schedule in New Orleans, where he is prepping for the upcoming *Wolverine* sequel. "I didn't know how I was going to go about that, but my transition into make-up came from animation. At the time, there were no schools on make-up. There were a couple of books and courses, but there was nowhere to really learn make-up except for experimenting in my parents' house and destroying my mother's kitchen.

"A lot of those techniques I picked up trying to get into stop-motion animation," he adds. "It was about creating puppets and armatures and acrylics. They were a lot of the same tools and techniques that easily translated into make-up and prosthetics, and that world of character creation."

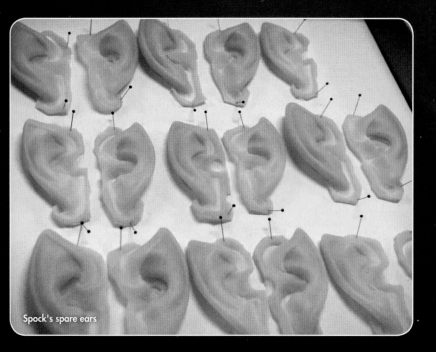

Spock's spare ears

"WE WERE ALL FANS OF *STAR TREK*. MORE THAN JUST HONORING THE SERIES AND THE FILMS, WE WANTED TO HONOR THE FANS. THAT'S WHAT WE ARE, TOO."

THE MAKE-UP OF A MAKE-UP ARTIST

Joel Harlow studied animation at New York's School of Visual Arts, before indulging his true passions for make-up and prosthetics by working on numerous low-budget horror and sci-fi movies. Developing his professional skills while creating innovative characters without breaking the bank, Harlow gained further experience working in various Hollywood make-up and effects studios over the next decade, before cementing his reputation with work on *How the Grinch Stole Christmas* and Gore Verbinski's *Pirates of the Caribbean* movies.

Harlow has been Johnny Depp's make-up artist on many of the star's biggest movies, and has worked with Oscar-winning directors Ron Howard (on *Angels and Demons*) and Christopher Nolan (on *Inception*).

Amongst many other prestigious awards nominations, Harlow won an Academy Award for his make-up work on J.J. Abram's *Star Trek (2009)*.

BEAMING BACK

Harlow is no stranger to the *Star Trek* universe. The 2009 reboot earned him an Academy Award. Unfortunately, Harlow was already committed to *The Lone Ranger* when *Star Trek Into Darkness* came around. However, when Bad Robot circled back for *Star Trek Beyond*, Harlow jumped at the chance to conceive and create more memorable aliens.

"In the beginning, typically how I approach any movie that has special characters in it, is we start with the design phase," he says. "That's not even specifically focusing on the scripted characters, but just the worlds in general. In a film like this, we had a bounty of opportunities. I hired a couple of designers. Together with my team, we just started designing the aliens. As things started coming together on the production end, and scenes were becoming clearer to us, we started slotting these aliens, with director Justin Lin's guidance, into various scenes.

"Certainly, we knew we needed to design Krall, Jaylah, and some of the lead alien characters," Harlow continues. "That was our focus. But, when you focus only on characters like that, you can overdesign them, unless you broaden your range and start designing the

whole thing. You never know when you are going to come up with an idea that works for one of these characters. That could come to you while designing something completely different. We hit it all at the same time. When Justin started approving designs – when he saw something in one of the designs that he thought would work for Krall, Jaylah, or whoever – he would let us know. Then we would design specifically those elements into our finished product."

CRAFTING KRALL

Harlow and his team fabricated hundreds of aliens from scratch, and transforming actor Idris Elba into the ruthless Krall proved to be one of the most challenging. As it turns out, Krall was a four-stage makeup character, which explains why Elba is virtually unrecognizable. In the movie, he goes from extreme alien, to something more human, as well as the two stages in between.

"When we designed him, I think we were initially going for the silhouette," Harlow offers. "My design aesthetic is if it doesn't work in silhouette, then all your details are forgotten. It's the broad strokes that are going

to bring people into the character, and it's the details that are going to keep them there. We design silhouettes first, and certainly he has a pretty powerful silhouette. And he's a powerful character. Those things tend to go hand-in-hand. Then, scaling him back towards human, it's a matter of incorporating human anatomy into what we have determined would be his full-blown alien look."

Elba's make-up sessions only lasted for approximately two hours, which is relatively short in comparison to what actors Ron Perlman and Doug Jones have endured in movies like *Hellboy*. Harlow notes there is a reason for that, especially on a film this scale, which requires 50 to 60 alien races.

"When you are designing that many characters, you have to design a lot of them generically, because you don't know the location," says Harlow, "Whether it was Vancouver, Dubai, Los Angeles, or wherever you are shooting – you are going to get actors and actresses that are local talent. You are

Keenser (Deep Roy) makes his comeback
(Image courtesy of Simon Pegg/Twitter)

going to have to make those prosthetics work on the people they send to you to play those characters. Typically, that takes longer.

"On somebody like Idris, who we knew was playing Krall, we could design it so we had a relatively minimum of amount prosthetics to achieve the look," he continues. "On Idris, he'd have a chin and an upper-face piece. On a generic, you'd have a chin, cheeks, a forehead, a nose and an upper-lip. There's considerably more involved, not only in the lab with molding and sculpting, but also in application. Each one of those edges where the prosthetics come together needed to be blended flawlessly."

BLACK AND WHITE

Another key make-up was Sofia Boutella's Jaylah. The goal was to give her a distinct appearance compared to her male counterpart, Krall. Harlow collaborated with a team headed up by make-up genius Neville Page to achieve that design.

> "MY DESIGN AESTHETIC IS IF IT DOESN'T WORK IN SILHOUETTE, THEN ALL YOUR DETAILS ARE FORGOTTEN."

"We knew she needed to be iconic more than anything else," Harlow explains. "That pale skin, black stripe look came from Joe Pepe, one of Neville's designers. It was something Justin gravitated towards during one of the meetings, which was great because it's instantly iconic. There's nothing more striking than black and white together. That character needed to be instantly recognizable and instantly iconic. That design is absolutely that. Then, translating it into a make-up, you run into a lot of hurdles to make something like that actually work. To

make those lines the same every time you apply it for 30 to 40 to 50 days is difficult."

Both make-ups proved to be labor-intensive undertakings. There are not only the prosthetics and paint jobs, but even initially nailing the correct shade of white for the skin color required some trial and error. Ironically, Harlow points out that tone isn't even white.

"It only reads white because that pale skin complexion is next to an absolute black color," Harlow states, "That contrast allows it to read whiter than it is. You can't go with something that is a traditional white because then it would look clown-like. There's a multitude of colors, granted they are all pale colors in that make-up, but the overall impression is white. In order to make it look like skin, we have to break it up as you would a traditional prosthetic. There was a lot of experimentation for what that color combination would be and in what order those colors would be applied. If you put one of those colors on before another, you get a different look.

One of *Star Trek Beyond*'s 50–plus alien races

shell. It's very beautiful. It was done on a young woman named Ashley Edner, who happens to be my stepdaughter, and has gone through the make-up process many times before, so I knew she could take it. It was probably our longest make-up appliance. Its full upper-body arms, head, and face. It took about six hours to apply.

"Any time you are designing a character, you've got to keep in mind that if you are going for something that is a prosthetic make-up, the reason to do it as a make-up is so that the performance can translate," adds Harlow. "Otherwise, you are dealing with a mask, whether it's mechanical or traditional. If you are doing it as a prosthetic, the trick is to keep it as thin as possible, so the performer's facial expressions can translate through. In this case, we were using silicon for our prosthetics."

There's no denying Harlow put countless hours of blood, sweat, and tears into *Star Trek*

"Same with Krall," continues Harlow. "He initially has a turquoise, pale-blue hue to him, almost a greyish-blue. There was a lot of experimentation as to what his skin tone would be. You don't want to go with something that people had seen before. You want the fans to be happy. We're creating new races of aliens, and you want fans to appreciate that. It was to read as real, but it has to read as alien, too. We went through a lot of different color tests with that make-up. As he gets more human, that make-up changes in color. Now, his natural skin tone is coming through in the make-ups as opposed to something completely alien."

NEW LIFE FORMS

It's not easy creating cool and innovative aliens. These days, everything seems to have been done. In order to get inspired, Harlow says they turned to nature.

"There's an aesthetic to the *Star Trek* universe and we didn't want to veer too far away from that," states Harlow. "But, we wanted to deliver something that hadn't been seen before. There's a wealth of alien designs on this planet already, whether it's deep sea or deep jungle or rain forest. There's a lot here to draw on. You start taking those elements and move them around, keeping in mind that most of them are going on human performers. That gives you an infinite number of possibilities."

On top of all the practical designs, Harlow acknowledges the movie features three or four animatronic characters, including a completely non-human creation. However, most of their workload was prosthetics-driven.

Krall's inricate prosthetics

"I don't want to speak out of turn, but this film has perhaps the largest number of different prosthetic characters in it that has been done in a long time, and perhaps ever," Harlow explains. "I say different prosthetic characters, because each one of these characters is its own unique design. It's not like doing a film with a bunch of goblins, and they are all very similar. These are all very different, and they all require different sculptures and different processes and molds. Some have larger heads, so they require engineering ways to keep the weight down without sacrificing the look. There are over 50 of them.

"There's one alien I'm particularly proud of," says Harlow. "That's an alien we refer to in the workshop as Natalia. That one is very ocean-life influenced. Its head is basically a nautilus

Beyond – and it shows. Although Harlow is justifiably pleased with how things turned out, he admits there was a lot of pressure to live up to everyone's expectations, including his own. "I had a crew of 30 in Burbank, another 35 in Vancouver, and another 15 in Dubai," Harlow. "We were all fans of *Star Trek*. More than just honoring the series and the films, we wanted to honor the fans. That's what we are, too. The pressure we put on ourselves to honor our audience, to honor the other fans of *Star Trek*, was greater than the pressure we felt to honor the other films. Every movie stands alone. It is *Star Trek Beyond*. It is its own entity. As long as Justin and production was happy, and J.J. Abrams was happy, we were happy. Hopefully that translates to the finished product." A

ANTON YELCHIN
CHEKOV

Returning to the role which made him a household name, the late Anton Yelchin's performance as Ensign Pavel Chekov in *Star Trek Beyond* further highlighted the much-missed actor's talents, with a finely judged balance of naiveté, strength, and humor.

Words: Bryan Cairns

Anton Yelchin as Chekov in *Star Trek* (2009)

Star Trek Magazine: You've been keeping busy since *Star Trek Into Darkness* beamed into theaters, but how eager were you to revisit Chekov, and to reunite with the cast?
Anton Yelchin: I always have a good time with those guys. The character is so much fun to play, so I'm always game for it. It's interesting, because I've never had the experience of making three films in a row with the same people, and, most importantly, the same character, before. I grow as I learn. How I look at my work has changed. Every time, I get to apply these new ideas to the same character. That's the thing that excites me the most, and to get to see those guys all together.

STM: How easy was it slipping back into Chekov's mindset, and nailing the accent and all his nuances?
AY: I sort of go back to the same thing every time. I watch the original series. That's my go-to source every time we've done the films, starting with the first one. I'll do that on my days off,

and try to apply that to what we're doing. There's a lot more Chekov in season three, so I wanted to focus on season three, even though I prefer seasons one and two in tone. Inevitably, I start drawing from other sources that I wasn't aware of when I was younger. I've been very fortunate to be playing this character, this joyous, fun role that Walter Koenig created. I'm indebted to him for setting me up in this great way. He crafted such a fun character, so I try and embrace that energy every time, and be respectful of that.

STM: As you mentioned, you've never stayed with a character this long before. In what ways has Chekov evolved between the 2009 reboot and *Star Trek Beyond*?
AY: Obviously, all these people have been on this journey for a few years. The first film was really about learning what their responsibilities are, coming out of school and going on this mission. Every film since then, especially this one, is about understanding what their duties are as part of this crew. That's my feeling I got from this film. It's really learning what the crew means to each other, and what their position in the crew means to them. It's an interesting, weird journey.

"THIS ONE BRINGS IT BACK A LITTLE BIT MORE TO THE HUMOR, JOY, AND ADVENTURE OF THE ORIGINAL SERIES."

Time for desperate measures, in *Star Trek Beyond*

STM: There must have been some anticipation before receiving the new script. What was your initial impression when you read it?
AY: I really liked it. I thought it was cool. I thought the ideas were exciting. It's hard, when you read scripts like that. There are pages of action, and you have no idea what they're going to look like. But I thought it was funny, and contained some wit and humor that, of course, Simon Pegg brings to it.

STM: From the previews, there seems to be more levity. Can you touch on the tone of this installment?

AY: The last film was very heavy. Even the title, *Into Darkness*, had that gravitas to it. This one brings it back a little bit more to the humor, joy, and adventure of the original series. That being said, there's still some pretty intense stuff in this one. I think the overall goal is to make it an adventure film. That's the feeling I got.

STM: Kirk and Chekov pair up for some shenanigans. What was fun about that dynamic, and in what ways did the characters surprise each other?
AY: Chekov turns out to be Croatian instead of Russian. Kirk can't believe it. No, that is *not* true. It's about finding out what each one can contribute. I had a lot of fun hanging out with Chris [Pine], and doing all this stuff. We've become buddies over the years, so it was a blast.

STM: Audiences have only been treated to snippets of Kirk and Chekov interacting. How did you guys gel?
AY: Chris is a funny dude. We laughed a lot. In general, we're a cast that laughs a lot. It's a little different from how I approach other characters. It's a little hard to stay in character with Chekov throughout, because he's so goofy. It's a cast that laughs at everything. My main take-away from shooting is how much we laugh at dumb stuff. John [Cho] and I break out laughing all the

time. We're always coming up with songs, and playing banjos.

STM: Chekov typically sits on the bridge or keeps busy in the engine room. How rewarding was it to get off the *Enterprise*?
AY: That was a blast. Last time, I was off the ship because I was on different sets, but I guess I was still technically on the ship. Chekov does get to [leave the ship] in the original series. I was happy to be able to do that in the movies, too.

STM: Chekov and many of the crewmembers sport new uniforms. Have his rank or responsibilities changed?
AY: Everyone in this movie takes on new responsibilities, by virtue of the situation they find themselves in. He hasn't switched, like in other films where he has a totally different position. That's not the case.

STM: *Star Trek Beyond* is the first time J.J. Abrams hasn't been behind the camera since 2009. What did new director Justin Lin bring to the table?
AY: Justin is very respectful of our dynamic, in terms of the actors. He's generous, and understands that there's going to be a dynamic

"THE CHARACTER IS SO MUCH FUN TO PLAY, SO I'M ALWAYS GAME FOR IT."

Chekov (Yelchin), Kirk (Chris Pine) and Sulu (John Cho) take control, in *Star Trek Beyond*

and a shorthand for all of us. Justin accepted that gracefully, and I appreciated that. I like seeing how different filmmakers work. There's a lot of effort going into this, and that was evident from day one.

STM: Justin certainly knows how to go full throttle. How much action does Chekov see in this film, and did you enjoy doing those beats?
AY: I did. It's always like being a little kid. It's an action film – I probably have more action than in any of the previous films. But I haven't seen the actual finished movie.

STM: Is it difficult to process how a film is going to turn out, when you're filming a sequence

> "I'VE BEEN VERY FORTUNATE TO BE PLAYING THIS CHARACTER, THIS JOYOUS, FUN ROLE THAT WALTER KOENIG CREATED."

with huge explosions, visual effects, and phaser blasts involved?
AY: Yeah, it's hard enough to process when there's a scene with two people at a table having coffee. So, when there's stuff that's not even there yet, it's challenging. You just connect to the reality of the emotion that you're supposed to be embodying. In terms of actually understanding what the hell is going on, it is challenging.

STM: What has this journey into *Star Trek* been like for you as an actor?
AY: We started so long ago. I've developed a different way to look at work, and what I was trying to accomplish. The more my perspective on the actual process changes, the more different ways I look at my own work. Even this time versus last time, I viewed things another way, and borrowed from different things. That being said, I always try and accomplish a similar character. You can see what you've learned about yourself every time you go to work. It's kind of odd, but I like it. ▲

ENTERPRISE NCC-1701
CREW MANIFEST

PAVEL ANDREIEVICH CHEKOV

Rank: Ensign
Position: Navigator
Species: Human
Date of birth: 2241
Place of Birth: Russia, Earth

Mathematically gifted, determined, and eager-to-please, Pavel Chekov was a child prodigy who was assigned to the *Enterprise* at the very young age of 17. Not only did he come top of his class in transporter theory, stellar cartography, and advanced theoretical physics, but Chekov was also the youngest cadet to win the Starfleet Academy marathon.
　　Although he can sometimes struggle to wrap his heavy Russian accent around Standard (English), Chekov never lets it stand in the way of getting results.

CHEKOV'S FINEST MOMENTS
Quick-thinking Chekov may seem naïve and even out of his depth, but the young Russian has an unerring knack for problem-solving...
* When Kirk and Sulu faced certain death falling into the singularity Nero created to destroy Vulcan, Chekov calculated their transporter beam coordinates quicker than the *Enterprise*'s computer (*Star Trek* (2009).
* Acting as Chief Engineer after Scotty resigned his position, Chekov was in the hot seat when an act of sabotage threw the *Enterprise* out of warp inside Klingon space.
* Repairing the *Enterprise*'s warp drive under extreme pressure, enabling the ship to escape an attack by the *U.S.S. Vengeance*.
* Restoring power to the *Enterprise* before it crashed into the Earth's surface, Chekov's

quick wits saved Kirk and Scotty from falling to their deaths as they raced to the warp core to perform emergency repairs (*Star Trek Into Darkness*).

"Ë MOË!"
("YO MOYO!", MEANING "OH MAN!")

BEYOND
STORYTELLING

Star Trek Beyond co-screenwriters Doug Jung and Simon Pegg share
their experience of scripting *Star Trek*'s latest big-screen adventure.
Words: Christopher Cooper

Things often change while a film is in pre-production, and they change fast. With a second sequel to J.J.Abrams' 2009 *Star Trek* movie set to shoot in June 2015, an overhaul of writing personnel in January of that year was a shock to everyone, not least those tasked with drafting the new film's script, from scratch.

Simon Pegg, already an old hand in the *Star Trek* universe, having played Scotty in Abrams' previous two movies, was teamed with Doug Jung, who had previously worked with Bad Robot on TV projects. The opportunity was as unexpected as it was welcome, for both writers.

"The screenplay for this *Star Trek* was underway, and pretty much taken care of," recalls co-writer Simon Pegg, who had originally thought he would simply be reprising his role as the *Enterprise* engineer for the movie, "so

when the decision came to reboot that process, it happened very quickly, as time was a factor. I didn't really have time to be as shocked as I should have been. I mean, in retrospect now, it should have been 'Wow', but it was a do-or-die moment, and you had to say, 'I'm in, or out.'"

For Pegg, the first indication that he was being sounded out came on the *Mission Impossible* set, through conversations with *Beyond* producer Bryan Burk.

"We were discussing *Trek*, and the notion of a different approach had come up, and I got the feeling that our conversations were a prelude to something like this," Pegg confides, "I think the decision by the studio was something they had to act on immediately, in order to continue the momentum."

Having written for Bad Robot previously, Doug Jung meanwhile believes his television

experience played a large part in being asked to join Pegg in scripting duties.

"I was in the middle of developing something for Bad Robot when it was suspended," says Jung, "and they asked if I would care to come on and help with *Star Trek Beyond*. In the most complimentary way, I took it that they understood me, and I understood how they worked, and with the constraints of the time period, maybe that was an asset for them.

"I did find that the skill-set that I had working as a writer and producer, doing stuff on TV, wasn't really applicable in a lot of ways," Jung continues, "but certainly the idea of working on something that big, and with people who are so on top of their game, was a really great learning experience for me."

With studios and cast already booked for the summer of 2015, the writing process was far shorter than would usually be the case for this scale of movie.

"It was an incredible amount of pressure," Jung admits, "to go from nothing, really, with the demands of having a script which you could prep off of in about four or five months. We needed to have very tangible, set ideas and specifics months before that. Normally, you get to have a draft that's very open to interpretation, and is going to be refined over three or four months, so the idea that we had to have something much more concrete is mildly insane."

"We had about six months before we started shooting," Pegg adds, "let alone pre-production, which is when everything gets designed and built, so you do need a certain amount of information going into a film in order to make it properly. We started from a blank page, and we never read Bob's [Roberto Orci, co-writer on the previous two movies] script until after the filming was complete. That was a decision that was made by the studio, in order to give us complete free rein. We just had to write quickly (Laughs)!"

That process began with a series of initial meetings between Pegg, Jung, Lindsey Weber [head of Bad Robot's film division], and director Justin Lin, to hammer out just what the movie would be about, as Jung explains.

"Broadly speaking, [we] talked about thematics that we thought would fit in, seemed appropriate, and really tried to say something about *Star Trek*, especially with the 50th anniversary coming up," says Jung, "And then we went through the messy process of trying to find out how to dramatize those ideas. That's when it gets like a crazy person's poster-board. Every thought, every idea, no matter how small, big, or insane, would go up, and then we would try to hone it down from there. It was ugly, but I think

Spock (Zachary Quinto) and McCoy (Karl Urban)

"WE HAD THIS REWARD FOR PUTTING IN HOWEVER MANY HOURS WE DID A DAY, WE'D WATCH AN EPISODE OF THE ORIGINAL SERIES IN SIMON'S SCREENING ROOM."

DOUG JUNG

Jaylah battles for her life, in *Star Trek Beyond*

SPOT THE WRITER

You'll get no prizes for spotting the red shirt of Simon Pegg as Scotty in *Star Trek Beyond*, but you will get kudos if you nail the character Doug Jung appears as in the movie…

"I actually do make a small cameo, but I'm not in a uniform," Jung reveals, "I can't say exactly what I'm doing, but it is in service of one of the other characters, and what we're saying about them, and who they are. I think it's going to be something that hopefully will be brought up a bit."

The thrill of appearing in a *Star Trek* movie does have its downsides, however, as Jung discovered…

"So, yeah, I got the really uncomfortable experience of being on a screen with incredibly good-looking, fit people, and not being one of them. I don't recommend it," laughs Jung, "They're like Greek gods. You want [Chris] Pine to be 5'5", but he's not, he's like 6'3" or something. Even Zac [Quinto], he's as tall as Chris, and Karl [Urban] is definitely pushing 6'2" or something. I mean, it's just ridiculous. There's no guys on apple boxes, which would have made the whole thing bearable.

Even John Cho, who's usually sitting down in these movies, he's not a short guy! You don't want to go out and eat a cheeseburger when you're hanging around them."

in this particular instance it was probably much uglier, just because, rather than trying to focus in on maybe the one or two key things, we had to do everything all at once."

"We just had to start answering questions quite quickly," Pegg agrees, "like, 'How many starships is that going to take?' and 'What does that look like?' In a way, that forced us to think on our feet, and to work smartly, and to not pontificate or procrastinate in any way. We didn't have the luxury of being able to chew things over for ages. We made decisions quickly, and, even though I wouldn't say it's an ideal way to write, in some respects it galvanized the process, and forced us to work intelligently."

Jaylah (Sofia Boutella)

GETTING TOGETHER

Known for his collaborations with director Edgar Wright (who was rumored at one point to be in with a shot at directing the *Trek* sequel), on films such as *Shaun of the Dead*, and the breakthrough TV comedy *Spaced*, Pegg found another kindred spirit in Doug Jung, despite the pair never having met before landing the *Trek* scripting gig.

"Fortunately, it worked out really well," Pegg reports of their working relationship, "We got along immediately. We obviously both had a shared love of the material, so we found that our intentions were pretty much exactly the same, in terms of what we wanted to create. That led to a fertile creative environment, because we were inspiring each other, and I think our game plan felt very much in tune with each other."

Jung traveled to London, and stayed with Pegg for several weeks to work on the screenplay.

"Doug came to stay with me in the UK, and we had a really good time. We worked really hard during the day, and then in the evening we'd sit and watch old episodes of the show," reveals Pegg, "taking notes on small details we thought we could seed into our screenplay, and it worked well. It was certainly not anticipated that it would be easy, but it was actually conducive to the process. We forged a friendship very quickly, and a way of writing, and I think that helped."

"We just camped out at Simon's lovely house, and it was great," Jung confirms, "It was the purest sense of writing something, because it was just Simon and I, and we had all these ideas – some of them were really good, some of them needed a lot of work – and we were on these really tight deadlines we'd set for ourselves. We had a real schedule of trying to get certain amounts of pages done, and certain acts done at certain times. We would sit in his office, with this beautiful English landscape outside, horses passing the window… it was so counter to what was going on in that room, with us furiously typing. We were riding on the seats of our pants doing this, but Simon was so great. It was really the most significant time we'd spent with each other too, so the fact that we got along so great was fantastic."

And as the duo got deeper into writing the script, the initial pressure they'd felt soon evaporated.

"We started getting into a groove where it got really fun for us, 'cause we were inventing things for each character that we loved," says Jung, "Every now and then we'd stop and [remember] 'we're writing this scene between Spock and Bones, or Kirk and Spock or whoever,' and – as tough as it was, as hard as it was – the fun of that was really infectious. We had this reward for putting in however many hours we did a day, we'd watch an episode of the original series in Simon's screening room, and that was our 'job well done' for the day. And we'd start all over again the next. It was really cool."

Bones (Karl Urban) gets in on the action

FAN ON THE BRIDGE

While Simon Pegg's geek credentials are writ large across his résumé, we were curious to discover Doug Jung's affinity for *Star Trek*...

"I love *Star Trek*," says Doug Jung, unable to hide his enthusiasm for the franchise, "I never had dreamed that I would ever be doing a *Star Trek* movie. I loved them so much, and I knew them pretty well – I didn't realize how well I knew them – and then you click over into that other headspace of, 'Now you have to write one!' It was really great.

"They were on late at night, on the syndicated channel where I grew up. I remember being just drawn in by them," Jung adds, "The great thing about *Star Trek* is that you have this nostalgic memory, and as you get older you start to really appreciate what they were doing on that show. You understand the lineage, whether it's the movies or the TV shows, the whole idea of what that Roddenberry universe is. It's one of those shows, for me, that has a unique perspective to it, which deepens as you get older. There's not many things, I think, you have that experience with."

"JUSTIN LIN WAS REALLY AT PAINS ON SET TO SAY 'I DON'T WANT THIS TO BE *FAST & FURIOUS* IN SPACE.'"

SIMON PEGG

GET SET, GO!

Principal photography took place between June and October 2015, with pick-ups the following March, and the writers were present throughout – with Pegg fulfilling his dual role as writer and performer.

"We were there on set pretty much every day," explains Jung, "Simon had to pull double duty at times, which must have been tough, but whenever we were together, I felt like things were really productive. We were moving so fast, the principal creative minds had to be constantly in communication with each other, even on the day, on the understanding that we had to be quick on our feet to make the changes that were needed."

For movie writers to be so heavily involved with day-to-day production is unusual, to say the least, and Jung was grateful for the opportunity.

"We worked really closely with the production heads, the production designer Tom Sanders, who was great, the art department, props, even the guy who invented all the alien languages, so I think Simon and I got a very unique perspective on tentpole movies, that will probably never happen again," Jung reflects, "Because of the circumstances, we were really in the fold with so many things that screenwriters don't usually get to do. For me, it was a totally unique thing to be working that closely with all those guys, on that level. It was tough, but at the same time incredibly rewarding."

Pegg adds, "Sometimes we'd say, 'This could happen,' and we'd get a flat, 'No, it would be too expensive or too time-consuming,' but I think necessity is always the mother of invention

Doug Jung

when it comes to writing. If you're given too much freedom, you'll often create just a big bowl of mess. I think sometimes having restrictions, having parameters, is really helpful."

ECHOES FROM BEYOND

As Pegg explains, the tight production schedule of the big-budget *Beyond* echoed some of the same constraints that were facing Gene Roddenberry and his team, as they made the (albeit less well-financed) original *Star Trek*, in the late 1960s.

"Back then, for different reasons, it created something which has lasted for 50 years. The limits that they had forced them to create the show that became so, so loved," says Pegg, "When it started, they had a certain amount of resources, and those resources tended to dictate the nature of the

shows. So what *Star Trek* was, and is, evolved out of the fact that they didn't have the capacity to make it spectacular, or depict the galaxy in the grandest terms, so they had to pull it into a very human story. By necessity, they built that show in such a way, that if they'd had all the money in the world, it might have become more frivolous and disposable. But because they were limited in what they could do, it became really cerebral, and really smart, and almost by accident became the brilliant thing that it is. Doug and I always said it's like watching a play, almost like a theatrical presentation of an interesting, philosophical idea."

With a teaser trailer that seemed to imply *Beyond* would, instead, be an all-action *Trek*, Pegg is keen to point out that the new movie steers much closer to the spirit of the original show.

Zoe Saldana as Uhura

New crew combinations, in *Star Trek Beyond*

> "WHAT *STAR TREK* WAS, AND IS, EVOLVED OUT OF THE FACT THAT THEY DIDN'T HAVE THE CAPACITY TO MAKE IT SPECTACULAR, OR DEPICT THE GALAXY IN THE GRANDEST TERMS, SO THEY HAD TO PULL IT INTO A VERY HUMAN STORY."
>
> **SIMON PEGG**

"Justin Lin was really at pains on set to say, ' I don't want this to be *Fast & Furious in Space*,' so it was really good to know that, despite his extreme adeptness with those kind of big set-pieces, we were able to place those original ideas and thoughts into something more spectacular and exciting. We came to it with a huge amount of love and respect, and that was always our main focus, not what the return was going to be on the movie, or how many bums would hit seats. For us it was just being true to *Star Trek*, and it being something we can be proud of." ▲

At the edge of the Federation, on the frontier between the known and the unknown, the crew of the *Enterprise* encounter a terrifying, unstoppable force, determined to push back...

With notes from co-writer Doug Jung, we set the scene for the latest chapter in *Star Trek*'s ongoing story.

Words: Christopher Cooper

INTO THE GREAT...

BEYOND

THE PLAYERS AND PLANETS OF *STAR TREK BEYOND*

The *Enterprise* crew seek out new life and new civilizations

THE *ENTERPRISE*

Captain James T. Kirk and his crew are two years into an unprecedented voyage through uncharted space. Along the way, they have made first contact between the Federation and numerous new alien races, leading to a rapid expansion in the Federation's sphere of influence.

But a five-year mission is a long time to be so far from home, where no one has gone before. As they push beyond a fiery nebula known as the Necro Cloud, it becomes clear that the crew are all-but exhausted.

In need of some shore leave, a visit to the *Yorktown* Starbase becomes a flashpoint that could undermine the future of the Federation.

U.S.S. Enterprise NCC-1701

THE UNITED FEDERATION OF PLANETS

Unique in our galaxy, the Federation is a grand interstellar experiment, an accord between an alliance of star systems to co-exist under a single, shared governing body, based on the tenets of equality, peaceful cooperation, exploration, and liberty.

Founded on Earth in the year 2161, the Federation grew out of the earlier "Coalition of Planets," a group comprised of Humans, Vulcans, Andorians, and Tellarites. With the addition of other races, including the Denobulans and the Rigelians, the Federation began a period of expansion that would soon see its peaceful ethos challenged by both the Klingon and Romulan Empires. Now, from the depths of beyond, the Federation faces a threat like nothing it has encountered before.

San Francisco, home to the United Federation of Planets

The Federation under attack, in *Star Trek* (2009)

BEHIND THE SCENES

"If you look at the Federation from one way, it seems very egalitarian and great. But if you look at it another way, you're talking about an organization that sweeps across the universe, trying to get as many people to join it as they possibly can. It's a matter of perspective. We wanted to add that sense of real politic."
DOUG JUNG

YORKTOWN STARBASE

Conceived as a place where the members of the United Federation of Planets can come together, to resolve differences or forge new friendships, the *Yorktown* Starbase is a glorious technological achievement. A hub for cultural exchange, at the very edge of Federation space, *Yorktown* serves a dual function as an open port to those interested in joining the Federation, as well as serving existing members and educating recent inductees.

However, its establishment has caught the attention of those who see it as an imperialist outpost of an expansionist regime – and its very location makes it a prime target for their anger...

The gleaming spires of the *Yorktown* Starbase

Krall's forces attack *Yorktown* in *Star Trek Beyond*

BEHIND THE SCENES

"Getting anybody together on the same page isn't an easy thing to do, so we originally thought of *Yorktown* as a place that was this great achievement, technologically, but it was also imbued with this sense of newness – I don't want to say instability but, you know, there was a delicacy to it, in a diplomatic sense, in a foreign relations sense, and that felt honest to us.

Again, it goes to that idea of, as different as we are on this planet, in the universe, in relation to other cultures and other belief systems, the drive to find a commonality is the thing that we should be honing in on, as opposed to focusing on our differences. That's a very Roddenberry idea that we tried to infuse the story with."
DOUG JUNG

KRALL

As it expanded across space, the Federation reached out with a hand of friendship to any willing to grasp it. The last thing it expected was to create an enemy more likely to rip that hand, and the arm it was attached to, clean off.

Krall is an unknown quantity with but one goal – to halt the inexorable advance of the Federation. For Kirk and the *Enterprise* crew, he is the most formidable foe they have yet encountered on their five-year mission, and by far the most deadly...

Kirk (Chris Pine) is up to his neck in trouble with Krall (Idris Elba)

Idris Elba as Krall

BEHIND THE SCENES

"With Idris Elba's character, we wanted to have a villain who felt bad and intimidating, but his character very directly comments on Kirk's storyline, and where he's going. Thematically, they are very tied to one another, without ever completely understanding why. He's got the classic *Star Trek* villain qualities to him, but a dynamic like that made him more interesting."
DOUG JUNG

JAYLAH

Feisty, determined, and ready to fight back, Jaylah has been stranded on the same world where the *Enterprise* crew find themselves – and she knows why they are there. No friend to Krall and his troops, Jaylah's help is indispensable to Kirk and his friends in their desperate struggle to survive in a hostile environment.

Jaylah (Sofia Boutella) takes on Krall's footsoldiers

BEHIND THE SCENES

"Sofia Boutella plays this totally new alien character, and she ended up being one of the best characters to write. Simon found a voice for her that was a bit of a wink and a nod to, 'Why is it, whenever they find aliens in the original series, they all speak English? What does that really say?' It's obvious why they did that back then, but now we have the technology to explain it in a better way.

"She ended up being this fun, wild card character, and great for us, because we got to add a new alien race to the canon." ⋀
DOUG JUNG

Sofia Boutella as Jaylah, in *Star Trek Beyond*

BORN INTO CONFLICT

DECONSTRUCTING KRALL

Balthazar Edison was a soldier, a warrior, during a period of galactic upheaval and war. But the conflict ended, and the universe span on – leaving the likes of Edison to find their place in a new galactic order of peace and cooperation, under the wing of the United Federation of Planets. With war in his blood, was his transformation into Krall inevitable?

Words: K. Stoddard Hayes

Krall (Idres Elba)

Krall first appears to the crew of the *Enterprise* as an unknown enemy with two alarming capabilities. First, the enemy has the knowledge and cunning to lay a trap that overwhelms a Federation starship. Second, they are in possession of weapons technology that literally tears the ship apart.

In the face of that terrifying, unknown technology, it must almost be a relief for Kirk to encounter the enemy leader face to face, and discover that he is just another humanoid, albeit a hugely strong one. A faceless enemy is impossible to grapple with. A humanoid alien with specific motivations can be understood, and possibly defeated.

The first thing the crew learns about Krall's motives is that he wants the alien artifact, the Abronath, desperately enough to destroy a starship to get it. He lures the *Enterprise* into his ambush in the nebula because the artifact is on board, and boards the ship himself to retrieve it. The usual villain motives become clear later, when he reveals that the object of his obsessive search is a key part of an ancient weapon, so dangerous that its inventors tore it apart and dispatched its pieces into deep space, hoping it would never be found.

Even at first encounter, Krall seems to take personal pleasure in destroying the starship, and in beating up her Captain. He appears to know a lot about the Federation, and even seems to be trying to understand his enemy's motivations, when he asks Uhura why she would sacrifice herself for her Captain.

More important, his need for the Abronath is directed specifically at the Federation. He wants it, his lieutenant, Kalara, explains, "to save you from yourselves."

If that sounds like the dogma of a fanatic, Krall soon makes it clear that the fanaticism is all his own. He despises the Federation and everything that it represents. Over and over again, he mocks the Federation and rages to his Starfleet adversaries that the Federation has made its people weak by forcing them into an artificial unity.

Peace and unity are "myths the Federation would have you believe," he says, and that the "Federation has taught you that conflict should not exist – but without struggle, you cannot know who you truly are."

After five decades of *Star Trek* idealism, it may be hard for us to understand how those ideals of interspecies peace and harmony can

"I AM A SOLDIER. THAT'S WHAT I WAS BORN INTO."

BALTHAZAR EDISON TIMELINE

- **Prior to 2153:** Balthazar Edison is born on Earth, receives military training, and becomes an officer in the MACOs (Military Assault Command Operations.)

- **2153 – 2154:** Edison serves with the MACOs in the Xindi War.

- **2156 – 2160:** Edison serves with the MACOs in the Earth-Romulan War.

- **2161:** Founding of the Federation; MACOs disbanded. Edison is transferred to Starfleet, and assigned command of the *U.S.S. Franklin*.

- **2164:** *U.S.S. Franklin* is caught in a wormhole anomaly and crash lands on Altamid. Edison and most of his crew survive, but are stranded. Starfleet lists the ship and crew as missing for the next 100 years.

- **Circa 2165:** Edison and his crew give up hope of rescue and turn to Altamid technology to prolong their lives. The technology transforms Edison into Krall and his officers into similar aliens. They master the Altamid drone technology, and plan a war of vengeance against the Federation.

- **2263:** Krall discovers that the Abronath is on the *Enterprise*. He destroys the ship, captures the Abronath, and uses the weapon to launch his long planned attack against Federation starbase *Yorktown*. He dies in hand-to-hand combat with Kirk, when he is sucked into space and consumed by the very bioweapon he coveted.

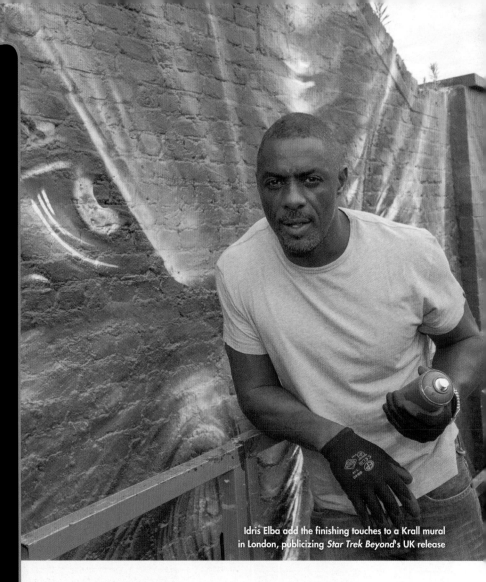

Idris Elba add the finishing touches to a Krall mural in London, publicizing *Star Trek Beyond*'s UK release

appear so destructive that the Federation's citizens need to be saved from them.

DIVERGENT IDEALS

Yet the Federation does not inevitably appear benevolent to others, especially its smaller and weaker neighbors. Nowhere is this clearer than in the Bajoran region in the Prime Timeline. The Federation's peace with Cardassia sacrifices the safety of a number of Federation colonies that have ended up in Cardassian territory. That treaty boundary, negotiated by the Federation and Cardassian governments, must have seemed brutally arbitrary to those colonists. The Maquis uprising was their response.

And as for the newly liberated Bajor, Kira tells Sisko to his face in *Deep Space Nine*'s pilot episode, "Emissary," that she opposes the provisional government's decision to call in the Federation's assistance.

"We're just here to help..." Sisko explains, to which Kira retorts, "That's what the Cardassians said 60 years ago."

Krall's grudge against the Federation is deep, bitter, and wholly destructive. He has spent decades searching for the Abronath, so that he can use it as a weapon to attack space station *Yorktown*, then use the station and its resources as a base from which to wipe out the entire Federation. It's not until this attack is already launched that the *Enterprise* crew finally discovers why.

In the video log of the *U.S.S. Franklin*, wrecked on Altamid 100 years previously, Uhura,

"YOUR UNITY IS NOT YOUR STRENGTH. IT IS YOUR WEAKNESS."

who now knows Krall well, recognizes him in the image and voice of Captain Balthazar Edison. The crew of the *Franklin* didn't die, at least not all of them. They used the ancient Altamid energy transference technology to prolong their lives – at the expense of their humanity.

And after years of waiting for a rescue that never came, Edison believed that the Federation had abandoned his crew to their fate. He had no way of knowing that the wormhole that wrecked *Franklin* had brought her so far from where she had disappeared, that no one even knew where to search for her. Nor perhaps, could he guess that the nebula outside entirely hid the wreck from any sensor searches or communications. He only knew that he and his crew had been left

> "FEDERATION HAS TAUGHT YOU THAT CONFLICT SHOULD NOT EXIST – BUT WITHOUT STRUGGLE, YOU CANNOT KNOW WHO YOU TRULY ARE."

to die, which is reason enough for a Captain to bear a grudge.

WAR AND PEACE

Edison wasn't always a Starfleet Captain, though. He served first for years as a MACO, Earth's elite military force – fighters so tough that Archer personally requested a detachment to join his mission against the Xindi. Edison fought in both the Xindi War and the Earth-Romulan War, and rose to Major in that service before the MACOs were disbanded. Perhaps he was something like *Enterprise NX-01*'s Major Hayes, whose laser focus on any potential threat, and on mission, security, and defense, could make Reed's security protocols seem relaxed.

So Edison was first and foremost a soldier, as he tells Kirk. Like the warmongering Klingon and Federation leaders of *The Undiscovered Country*, he has always defined himself by his ability to fight against all enemies of Earth. Then Earth becomes a founding member of

Idris Elba at the UK *Star Trek Beyond* premiere

IDRIS ELBA

London-born Idris Elba paid his acting dues with years of work in small roles on British television, before being cast in his breakout role as drug dealer Stringer Bell in *The Wire*. Elba is best known as antihero detective *Luther* – a role for which he has won a Golden Globe, SAG, BET, NAACP and Critics Choice awards, and the actor was recently awarded an OBE.

Sci-fi and fantasy fans love him for a long list of badass characters, like Heimdall in the *Thor* movies, Stacker Pentecost in *Pacific Rim*, and of course, Krall. Whether playing hero, villain or something in between, he is always a formidable and fascinating presence. Elba will soon be seen conquering yet another epic fantasy role, as Stephen King's iconic Gunslinger, Roland Deschain, in the film adaptation of *The Dark Tower*. Elba has also done plenty of voice work, including voicing Shere Khan in Disney's live-action remake of *The Jungle Book* (2016), and he sidelines as a DJ and music producer.

EDISON BELIEVED THAT THE FEDERATION HAD ABANDONED HIS CREW TO THEIR FATE.

the Federation, and the MACO commander is suddenly expected to exchange his loyalty to Earth for allegiance to a new, interplanetary alliance. And he is asked to give up his life – his identity – as a soldier in the forefront of battle, and become an explorer and diplomat.

That is, apparently, more than he can easily accept. Invoking the millions lost in the Xindi and Romulan wars, he demands, "And for what? For the Federation to sit me in the Captain's chair, and break bread with our enemies?"

His role has shifted from being the front line of steel in battle against ferocious enemies, to being the man who just sits in the big chair and gives orders. That alone must be hard for a self-identified soldier to accept. It's a reduction of his personal power, similar to the feeling of uselessness the older Kirk of the Prime timeline experiences when he is an Admiral without a ship.

To make it even worse, Edison's orders are no longer about battle and defense. He's now an officer in a service whose main mission is not warfare but exploration. And after years of warfare, the enforced peace of the Federation does not seem to him to be admirable; it seems contemptible, a threat to human strength and courage.

SURVIVAL OF THE FANATICIST

Perhaps if Edison and his crew had been rescued from Altamid, he might have been able to make the adjustment to life as a Starfleet Captain under the Federation. But after half a human lifetime as a soldier, being first diminished to the role of peacekeeper, then being marooned and abandoned was too much.

Many military forces have a code of "leave no-one behind." For Edison, the abandonment by the Federation is the ultimate, intolerable betrayal. It must seem the final proof of his growing belief that the Federation's values are destructive to the strength of independent Earth, and worse, that those values are hypocritical. A state that does not value its soldiers and their sacrifices is surely not worthy of a soldier's loyalty.

Add to the shipwrecked captain's isolation and hardship a few decades of alien biological alteration, and Edison's belief in the Federation's betrayal and unworthiness becomes Krall's fanatical conviction that the Federation is a threat to human strength and evolution. And so Krall makes his plan to destroy the Federation, to make way for a world where one must be strong to survive.

And now we understand why his plan to send Kalara to *Yorktown* as a shipwrecked space traveler is so masterly. He grasps his enemy's weakness perfectly. Starfleet and the Federation, so eager to be benevolent, will immediately send their finest ship into a dangerous nebula to the rescue of Kalara's supposed crew, and they will never once consider whether this appeal for help might be a trap. This benevolence, too, must have seemed a bitter grievance: the Federation which abandoned his crew will risk a starship to rescue a crew of strangers.

And it works. The Federation values of unity and compassion not only bring the *Enterprise* within striking distance, they even provide him with the hiding place of the Abronath, when Ensign Syl gives it up rather than let him kill Sulu.

"Your unity is not your strength. It is your weakness," Krall spits, contemptuously.

However, that perspective becomes a blind spot when it prevents him from planning for the unity of his enemies. It's unity that drives Kirk and his officers to rescue every one of their surviving crew, plus their fellow castaway, Jaylah. This gives them all the hands they

need to get *Franklin* into the sky again, and to broadcast the "classical music" weapon that takes down Krall's drone fleet.

By the time Krall reaches *Yorktown* in the wreck of his last drone ship, his consumption of human life energy (harvested from more unfortunate members of Kirk's crew) has reversed his alien appearance so that he is restored almost completely to his human form. And it's to Edison, in his human form, that Kirk makes his final appeal, captain to captain.

"You won the war. You gave us peace," Kirk reasons.

Perhaps Edison has been too long in the form and the mind of Krall to abandon his vengeful war after a few moments of debate. It is so long since he has felt part of the human race, that he never had a hope of being won over by the persuasions of a human Starfleet Captain.

More likely though, as his history and his own logs indicate, he never believed in the values Kirk appeals to. Kirk's very idealism is an affront to him.

"Peace is not what I was born into!" he shouts back.

What does Krall/Edison see in that last moment, when he is floating up behind Kirk and catches sight of his own face, reflected in a shard of glass? Does he, perhaps, see the human he once was, the self he lost a hundred years ago?

No, the reflection makes him fly at Kirk in a rage. More likely, what he sees is a Starfleet officer, a representative of the hated Federation. The Federation peace is weakness, so the Federation must be destroyed. A soldier to the end, Krall dies trying to destroy the enemy who destroyed his life. ▲

Idris Elba at the San Diego world premiere after party

THE INSANITY OF COMMAND

Rogue Starfleet captains and commanders are all too familiar in the *Star Trek* universe. Kirk alone has encountered three other rogue Captains, and two rogue Admirals across the original and *Kelvin* timelines.

COMMODORE MATT DECKER
"THE DOOMSDAY MACHINE"
A model commander, Decker was driven mad by a Captain's worst nightmare: the loss of his entire crew while he stood by, powerless to help. He hijacked the *Enterprise* in a suicidal attempt to destroy the planet killer, then flew a stolen shuttlecraft into it – and with his death revealed the key to destroying it.

CAPTAIN RONALD TRACY
"THE OMEGA GLORY"
Tracy also lost his entire crew, to a biological weapon his landing party accidentally carried to his ship. Stranded on the planet, he threw away the Prime Directive and supplied phasers to one side in a centuries long civil war. He was arrested after Kirk made peace with the victorious leader of the opposing side.

GARTH OF IZAR
"WHOM GODS DESTROY"
A hero of Starfleet, Garth was healed from devastating injuries by alien cellular metamorphosis that, as a side-effect, drove him insane. When Kirk encountered Garth in a remote rehabilitation colony, he had styled himself "Lord Garth, Master of the Universe," and nearly succeeded in hijacking the *Enterprise*. Luckily, prospects for a new treatment look promising.

ADMIRAL CARTWRIGHT
THE UNDISCOVERED COUNTRY
ADMIRAL MARCUS
INTO DARKNESS
Both admirals lost sight of Federation ideals and tried to start a perpetual war with the Klingons. Since Kirk and Khan stopped Marcus's warmongering, early in the *Kelvin* timeline, it's possible that Cartwright's later attempt will never arise within that timeline.

EVENT HORIZON

High-profile marketing events play a massive part in the release of any big-budget movie, but *Star Trek Beyond*'s promotional campaign kicked off in unique style, on May 16th, 2016.

An unprecedented event treated a select throng of lucky fans to the launch of the movie's full trailer – and threw in a host of other treats too.

Words: Larry Nemecek

J.J. Abrams

t had been a long wait for fans to get a proper peek at Justin Lin's *Star Trek Beyond*. An early, action-heavy teaser trailer, released while *Star Wars: The Force Awakens* was setting pulses racing in cinemas, was clearly aimed at grabbing the attention of that audience – but it left some fans wondering whether this was *Star Trek*, or something else entirely?

The truth is, *Beyond* is purest *Star Trek*, and then some…

Lin and Paramount Pictures were keen to put that message out there, but how best to share their faith? How could they jump-start a media buzz while assuring fans that this new chapter, released in *Star Trek*'s 50th anniversary year, would indeed be the real deal?

The answer? By bringing them together at a grand unveiling of the movie's full trailer, at a swanky Hollywood bash starring producer J.J. Abrams, director Justin Lin, and the NuTrek triumvirate of Chris Pine, Zachary Quinto, and Karl Urban.

Scott Martin, of Sacramento, loved the secrecy surrounding the event: "I loved the surprises, and loved not knowing what to expect."

Zachary Quinto

(Left to right) Karl Urban, Chris Pine and Zachary Quinto entertain the crowd

"I flew in just for this event, and I think it is beyond amazing!" said an excited **Doyle Zhang** from Shanghai, a young woman who'd just won alien warrior Jaylah's screen-used stunt staff. "At first I thought it was just going to be a trailer, but we got to see footage, and I especially love the tribute for Leonard Nimoy. It's very touching."

One thousand attendees, including lucky, ticket-winning fans, *Trek* bloggers, news media, and celebrities – plus, thanks to live-streaming, a much larger, worldwide audience too – were invited to the Paramount lot for an event that caused an internet meltdown.

Beyond the thrilling new trailer came many other delights. A Q&A with stars Pine, Quinto, and Urban was a big hit, as was the chance to snag +1 passes to the movie's July 20th world premiere, revealed to be taking place at an outdoor IMAX theater during San Diego's famous Comic-Con.

A mass toasting took place, outside the 1960s soundstages where the original *Star Trek* was filmed, as an avenue was officially renamed as "Leonard Nimoy Way," in tribute to the late Spock actor. It was clear that everyone in attendance couldn't help but be swept up in an unexpected wave of excitement, reveling in *Star Trek*'s history, while looking forward to its bright tomorrow. ⏶

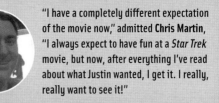

"I have a completely different expectation of the movie now," admitted **Chris Martin**, "I always expect to have fun at a *Star Trek* movie, but now, after everything I've read about what Justin wanted, I get it. I really, really want to see it!"

Karl Urban takes questions

"Amazing!" is how **Elise Cutts**, a CalTech student from Portland, Oregon, put it. "We got to see the whole scene with Bones and Kirk – deep and personal, contemplative – but then we got the ship blowing up, too. It has that fast pace you'd expect, but at the same time it has the heart."

Kirk actor Chris Pine

Leonard Nimoy's family honor his memory

Charles Baxter of Hesperia, California, a "fan for about 43 years," was grateful for the rare chance to hear Justin Lin's plans first hand. "I don't buy into the preconceptions of what a director has *done*," said Baxter, "I wait to see what a director *can* do. And that's what's more important."

University of Maryland chemistry major, **Tori Novato**, echoed the upbeat mood of the crowd – about the movie, and the historic night as well: "It's so the *Star Trek* we knew, but treated like it's still something new."

Fans gather for the new trailer

SHOHREH AGHDASHLOO

COMMODORE PARIS

As the commanding officer of Federation Starbase _Yorktown_, the intergalactic melting pot firmly in Krall's firing line, Shohreh Aghdashloo exudes calm authority under extreme pressure. For Aghdashloo, it was a small role that fulfilled a big dream.
Words: Ian Spelling

After a film completes principle photography and sets up for scheduled re-shoots – often involving simple pick-up shots to tighten the beats in a movie – it's rare to add an Oscar-nominated actress to the cast. However, that's exactly what happened when director Justin Lin and producer J.J. Abrams reassembled their cast and crew to shoot additional scenes for _Star Trek Beyond_, and tapped the talents of the Iranian-American star

of _House of Sand and Fog_, Shohreh Aghdashloo, to take a pivotal role in the journey of one James Tiberius Kirk.

Aghdashloo, who also appeared in the likes of _24_, _The Stoning of Soraya M_, and _The Expanse_, signed on to portray new character Commodore Paris, of Federation High Command. Commodore Paris may or may not be related to _Star Trek: Voyager_'s Tom Paris and Admiral Owen Paris, but she's the figure in _Beyond_ who assigns Kirk his life-changing mission, and welcomes him back upon its completion, along the way prodding him to reconsider his request to assume a desk job as vice admiral within the Federation.

Having grown up in Iran watching the original _Star Trek_ in Farsi with her brothers, Aghdashloo was already a fan, and brought great gravitas to the role, which felt like anything but an afterthought.

"I could not believe it, when I got the call about _Beyond_, to be honest with you," the actress says, "Being a fan, and then all of a sudden being a part of it, it was shocking, especially because it came together in a couple of days. I was in Toronto getting ready for

Aghdashloo's Paris plays an integral part in Kirk's (Chris Pine) journey

"BEING A FAN, AND THEN ALL OF A SUDDEN BEING A PART OF IT, IT WAS SHOCKING."

Aghdashloo refined her character via emails with director Justin Lin

my TV series, *The Expanse*, to shoot our second season. I like to be out there early, because I want to get used to the climate, and get myself ready. I like to live for a couple of days with my character, take my character to bed with me, you know? I like to get close to my character. So that's why, if I'm shooting on a location, I need to be there a week before – or at least a couple of days ahead.

"So, I was getting myself ready for *The Expanse*, and my agent called and said, 'You've been offered this role in *Star Trek*,'" Aghdashloo continues. "I'll never forget it. I said, 'Which one?' He said, '*Star Trek*.' I said, 'Did you say *Star Trek*?' He said, 'Yes, *Star Trek*.' I said, 'That one is finished.' He said, 'Yes, it's finished – but now they're doing more work on it, and they've decided to give you this role.' Apparently, I think it was Mr. J.J. Abrams who decided to do this, to add this powerful female role."

THERE ARE NO SMALL ROLES

Commodore Paris embodies the virtues of the United Federation of Planets, and plays a major role in shaping Kirk's decisions as to his future. Aghdashloo concurs with the suggestion that, for a relatively small part, Paris is a hugely important figure, and serves a major function within the story.

"Absolutely," Aghdashloo enthuses, "It's huge. Was it Norma Desmond who said that 'there are no small roles, only small characters?' It is very true. It doesn't matter how small the part is, it's one of the most important roles in the movie. She's not only trying to make the right decision for Starfleet and the Federation, but she also has to consider the feelings that she

Commodore Paris (Aghdashloo) commands Starbase *Yorktown*

has for [Kirk]; it's like a mother for her son."

Aghdashloo compares how Paris feels about Kirk to how "a mother country feels for her soldiers."

"When I was looking at him coming towards me," Aghdashloo explains, "and I was about to tell him, 'It's not just a ship that I'm sending, captain,' meaning that you have to be in it, too, I was thinking, 'Oh my God, this is Mother Earth, the motherland that is sending her soldier to war,' and her feelings are so mixed. She loves him as much as if he were her son. And also she loves him because he's an amazing captain, and

she relies on his expertise, and she has to send him on this very risky mission. Therefore, there are all these mixed feelings, and the connection between the two of them.

"And also, for me, I have to tell you, being from the Middle East, every time I read anything that's science fiction or futuristic, that are contemporary stories, what I inevitably try to do is find the metaphors and decode them," she adds, "That makes the stories even more

"IT DOESN'T MATTER HOW SMALL THE PART IS, IT'S ONE OF THE MOST IMPORTANT ROLES IN THE MOVIE."

delicious to me, personally, because in my mind I have metaphors, I have replacements for all the metaphors, and it makes it a lot more delicious and sweet for me to act it out."

THE PRIME DIRECTOR

The actress spent most of her time on *Beyond* collaborating with Justin Lin and Chris Pine. Much of Aghdashloo's interactions with Lin involved conversations and emails about Commodore Paris's motivations, and also the Prime Directive. With Pine, it was all about finding the spark of chemistry that would enable the audience to buy into the mother/son relationship.

"There were a lot of e-mails with Justin," Aghdashloo reveals, "I wrote one saying, 'Nobody

"WHEN I CAME TO THIS COUNTRY, 28 YEARS AGO, I WAS HOPING FOR THE DAY THAT WE COULD ALL TELL THE STORY TOGETHER. AND IT'S HAPPENING NOW."

can read the entire script, so I was wondering if you could help me out.' [Lin] gave me a couple of notes about the character, and then I started doing my research. The most important one of all was the notion of war by Plato, which I sent to Justin in an email, stating, 'Look, while I was doing my research, I came across this notion of war by Plato.' And Justin's answer was interesting. He said, 'You got it. I don't think you need me to tell you anything more. Just come and do it.' I said, 'OK.' I was so happy."

Comfortable with her director, Aghdashloo was also impressed by Chris Pine.

"I loved working with him," Aghdashloo says of Pine, "What a nice gentleman. Usually, you're afraid that because they are young, and because they are stars, not only actors, you don't know what you're going to get."

It was an experience that even made her daughter jealous.

"My God, my own daughter, she calls me and says, 'Shame on you. I have to find out you're in *Star Trek* through the internet?' I said, 'Tara, sweetheart, I just got the offer.' So, my daughter was upset with me. Then she said, 'I want to see him.' I said, 'You can't. We're filming in L.A.'

Shohreh Aghdashloo at the *Beyond* world premiere

SHOHREH AGHDASHLOO

Internationally renowned actress Shohreh Aghdashloo was born in Tehran, Iran, in 1952. Achieving recognition as a stage actress in the 1970s, her first major film roles (*The Report* and *Shatranje Bad*) brought her critical acclaim, but both were banned in her home country. When Iran became convulsed by a revolution in 1979, Aghdashloo moved to England, where she studied for a degree in International Relations.

Relocating to Los Angeles, Aghdashloo pursued her acting career on stage and television throughout the 80s and 90s, but it was her Oscar-nominated role alongside Ben Kingsley in *House of Sand and Fog* (2003) that made her name in Hollywood.

Chrisjen Avasarala – *The Expanse* (2015-16)
Stefania Vaduva Popescu – *Grimm* (2013-14)
Sajida Khairallah Talfah – *Flashforward* (2009)
Dr. Kavita Rao – *X-Men: Last Stand* (2006)
Dina Araz – *24* (2005)

Shohreh Aghdashloo as Commodor Paris, in *Star Trek Beyond*

Kirk (Chris Pine) is "like a son" to Commodore Paris

She said, 'Oh my God, you're going to have to tell me and all of my girlfriends about him.'

"So I'd go and start working with him every morning at 5am," Aghdashloo continues, "Around noon on the first day, when we broke for lunch, I had like 15 emails, 16 text messages. 'How is working with him? How does he look? Blah, blah, blah.' And then I called my daughter, and said, 'He's one of the most-handsome men I've ever seen in my life. And he's one of the most generous, and kindest, and nicest young men I've ever seen in my life.' All of her girlfriends were there, and they were all like, 'Oh my God, oh my God, I want to see him. I want to see him.' I really had a great time with Chris."

OPENING DOORS

Aghdashloo has enjoyed a long and prosperous career, first in her native Iran, before working in England, and finally settling in the United

States. It's an understatement to say that she's opened many Hollywood doors for other actors of Middle Eastern descent, and she's done it by portraying every kind of character: powerful and put-upon, villains and every-day women, working-class and in-charge.

"You know, usually I shy away from boasting about myself, but proudly I have to say that, yes, you are right," Aghdashloo admits. "It has made a huge difference, especially for the Iranian and Middle Eastern actors. The industry knows that we can act, too, let's put it that way. A friend of mine had gone to an audition, and she said, 'After I did my audition, I was leaving and the casting director said, "Wait a second, did you say you're from Iran?"' And my friend said, 'Yes, I'm Iranian.' And the casting director said, 'Like that Iranian actress?' And she said, 'Yes.' And the casting director says, 'Come back, do another one for me. I'll give you another chance.'

"I just loved it when my friend called me," the actress says. "I got a chill, and was so happy because this is what I wanted, what I was hoping for, from the beginning. When I came to this country, 28 years ago, I was hoping for the day that we could all tell the story together. And it's happening now, more and more, in terms of diversification. We see all these faces from all over the world, the Far East, India, New Zealand, Australia, everywhere. The last few projects I have done, I've worked with actors from all over, which is amazing. It's getting better and better. It's just fantastic."

Director Justin Lin

Aghdashloo grows reflective for a moment.

"When I was young, my grandmother whispered into my ear on a daily basis, 'A life without service is not a life.' Therefore, everything I do I'm hoping that I'm giving service to somebody, somewhere. Some people, some nations," she says. "I did this play, *White Rabbit, Red Rabbit*, in New York. After the play was done, I came out and this young American guy, tall and handsome, looked at me in awe and said, 'I am proud of you.' I had tears in my eyes and said, 'Oh my God, thank you so much. You've just made my evening.' He said, 'You made my evening. You did a great job.' I said, 'No, the play on its own was an amazing experience, but what you just told me made my entire month.' That feeling that an American man is proud of me? It was amazing, and it still is."

Shortly before *Star Trek Beyond* debuted in cinemas, worldwide, Paramount Pictures announced that it had greenlit a fourth film featuring the current *Enterprise* crew. It's not beyond the realms of possibility that Aghdashloo could wind up reprising her role as Commodore Paris sometime in the near future. If the opportunity presents itself, then count her in.

"Oh my God, I would jump up and leave home and join them!" Aghdashloo exclaims. "Oh my God, yes. Of course. Who doesn't want to be a part of such an amazing, amazing project?" ⋀

Paris (Aghdashloo) sends the *Enterprise* on a dangerous rescue mission (*Star Trek Beyond*)

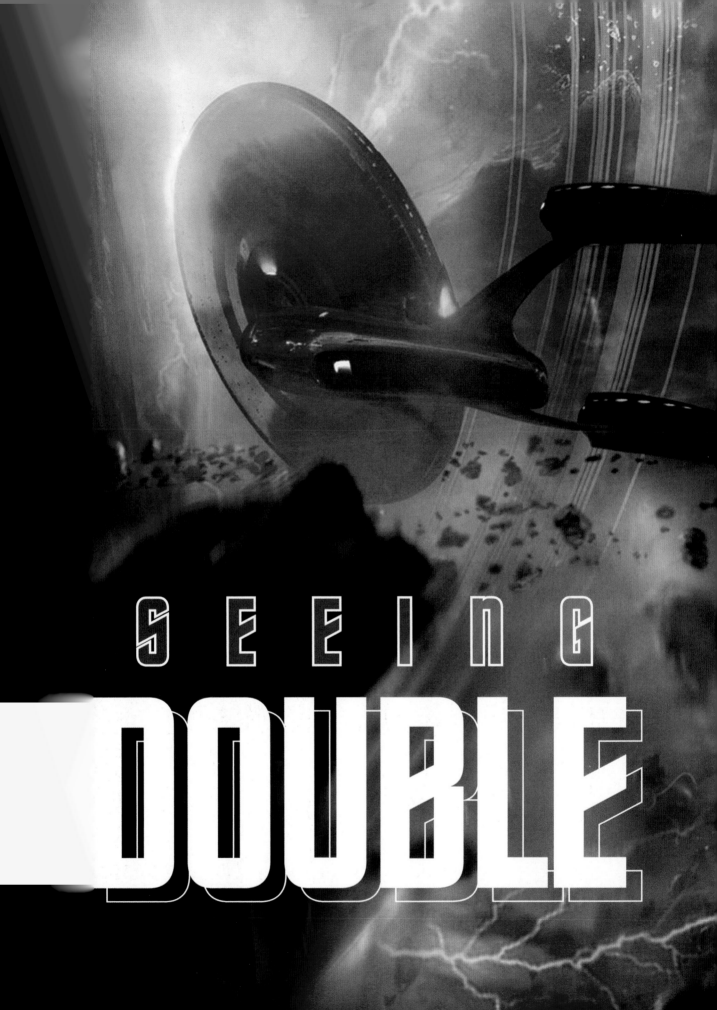

SEEING
DOUBLE

With a new director in Justin Lin, *Star Trek Beyond* was always going to have a different look and feel to what had gone before. The challenge facing Pete Chiang – VFX Supervisor on the movie and co-founder of Oscar-winning VFX company Double Negative – was to channel that new aesthetic into stunning effects that remained true to *Star Trek*'s visual lexicon.

WORDS: CHRISTOPHER COOPER

tar Trek Beyond opens with an iconic shot of the *Enterprise* orbiting a distant world. Kirk is on a diplomatic mission, brokering a peace deal with the fearsome (and quite belligerent) Teenaxi... and then the rug gets pulled – the Teenaxi aren't huge but teeny tiny! This sudden inversion of what the audience had been led to expect is a crazy visual gag that shouldn't work, but does, thanks to a combination of clever editing and subtle VFX.

"We shot on a bowl set in Vancouver, designed to have a forced perspective," explains Pete Chiang, the VFX Supervisor on *Star Trek Beyond*. "We were trying to sell multiple points of view in order to sell the scale, so the editors cut between Kirk on the pedestal and the alien [leader]. They're mirrored, so we've got a medium shot of Kirk, we cut to a medium shot of the alien. We do a front three-quarter of the alien, mid-height, and we do a front three-quarter of Kirk."

The reveal relies on this cinematic convention, that's almost as old as cinema itself, to mislead the audience into thinking that Kirk is about to be pummeled by the bulky Teenaxi. "Your subconscious perceives their size to be exactly the same," Chiang continues, "It's very subtle, but the depth of field in the CG rendered shots is slightly shorter than on the Kirk [live-action] shots. The Teenaxi is shot, digitally, on a wide angle lens to make him look big, but as we pull back to the feet of Kirk, there's a change to a longer lens."

The scene represents the visual complexity behind an apparently straightforward comedy moment, and is indicative of the attention to detail Chiang and his team at Double Negative put into every shot of *Star Trek Beyond.* The overall desire is to ensure digital and live action elements work together so seamlessly that audiences don't give it a second thought.

The unrendered but complex digital model of *Yorktown*

An exterior shot of *Yorktown* starbase, from *Star Trek Beyond*

YORKTOWN NIGHTS

Chiang, who began his film career as a graphics artist on *Krull*, has been a visual effects supervisor since the mid-90s, on features including *The Borrowers*, *Elizabeth*, and *Pitch Black*. From painting miniatures for effects legend Derek Meddings to putting the digital scales on *Godzilla*, Chiang's expertise is second to none, so what's his first move towards making the unreal real?

"Its easier to start off with something live action in the scene. There's a human element about me photographing you," says Chiang. "When shots wander too far away from being grounded by a bit of reality in the foreground, that's when they start to look hokey. And that's why I think Justin's approach of wanting to shoot something live, going to Dubai and having that as a representation of Starfleet, was a good idea."

Of all the new worlds realized for *Star Trek Beyond*, the Federation Starbase *Yorktown*, with its striking, soaring architecture, is by far the most ambitious (see sidebar). Every aspect of its function was considered, even down to the comfort of it's fictional inhabitants, and Dubai's hazy atmosphere – as captured during live-action shoot – fed into the eventual on-screen look.

TRANSPORTER TROUBLE

Adding to *Star Trek*'s long and rich visual history demands a close attention to what has gone before, and the transporter effect was no exception. Chiang was very mindful of this during pre-production, and the challenge of making the beaming-up process recognizable while bringing something new to the table.

"I've got a quick-time [video] of every transporter that's ever been done that just shows the different..." Chiang launches into a pitch-perfect vocalization of the beaming effect, "How they did the beaming stuff on *Voyager*, the first *Motion Picture*, the 'spaghetti' from J.J.'s films. We very much wanted it to be particle-based, so I was looking at exploding paint and exploding powder. We imagined the particles swirling together and falling, because it's breaking up, so if you look at the effect, there's a particle system that's not just all glowing lights. It's actually forming shapes and pulling it together."

While the *Enterprise* transporter was a mix of the familiar with a sprinkling of the new, the *Franklin*'s cargo transporter needed a different look.

"It took a while to get there, actually," says Chiang, "The story point of the *Franklin* was [that] it's a cargo transporter, and Scotty's rigged it up to transport people. We wanted it to be unstable, so that it adds to the jeopardy. At one point we said let's just go back to the 60s, lets just do that matte shape with the texture on the inside, and modernize it, so we played around with it but it just wasn't aesthetically as pleasing. It didn't feel modern enough to be different, to be from the *Franklin*."

The *Franklin*'s transporter in action

"JUSTIN WAS JUST SO KEY TO GETTING IT SHAPED THE WAY THAT HE WANTED, AND I THINK THAT HIS PASSION AND KNOWLEDGE OF *STAR TREK* REALLY SERVED."

TREK TRIVIA: YORKTOWN

Concept art of *Yorktown*

The digital *Yorktown* model was built at a real world scale, with a 16-mile diameter, and the same model was used for both the outer space shots and the climactic chase scenes at street level (and beneath). The entire build for *Yorktown* was made up of 1.3 trillion polygons, with over 800 unique assets, from the 8-mile long city-arms down to individual lamp posts.

Chiang explains how the VFX incorporated the dusty skyline of Dubai into their alien environment. "We played up the haze as atmosphere, so it's like sky. We had *Yorktown* as hazy during the day, as you'd want the people to feel as though they're on a planet. You don't want them to feel too disorientated."

Night on *Yorktown* offered a different challenge for the VFX crew. The initial idea was that when Spock receives the news of Old Spock's death, and looks out towards the night sky, he would "see the galaxy." It took several attempts to get the shot right.

"There's one point we went too far," laughs Chiang, "We had a magnificent galaxy outside, but somehow it looked like Spock was standing in a planetarium. It didn't look real, so we tempered it back to just a few stars at the top."

ALTAMID APOCOLYPSE

The other major environment created for the movie was Krall's alien stronghold, on the planet Altamid, which was shot on a very down-to-Earth location in Pit Meadows, just outside Vancouver.

"It was a quarry," admits Chiang, recalling that while the structure was perfect for the movie, it needed to look more alien. "Tom Sanders (production designer on *Beyond*, whose previous work includes *Apocalypto*), ended up spraying the rocks blue. I mean, you're painting a quarry that's about half a mile long, it's huge. And, in Vancouver it rains a lot."

With a newly redecorated quarry providing the physical location for Krall's base, the surrounding scenery was digitally extended to create a nightmarish range of jagged mountains. These were inspired by an astonishing geological landscape, located in the remote reaches of Canada's Nahanni National Park Reserve.

"We went to the Cirque of the Unclimbables, in the Yukon, to grab photographic reference of rock structures," recalls Chiang. In fact, gathering this

"WE DIDN'T WANT TO GO LENS FLARES, BECAUSE THAT'S J.J."

The rocky Pit Medows quarry set that doubled for planet Altamid

The *Franklin* decloaks amid the jagged Altamid landscape

Journey's end for the *Franklin*

RESCUE RESIN

One tricky piece of *Trek* tech to visualize was Jaylah's security system – that smoke-to-resin blob that captures Kirk and Chekov, and later protects the *Enterprise* crew from drone-lasers.

"That's the thing that I felt was one of the hardest effects we had to do, because everything in *Trek* is a bit real, there's a kind of a non-fantasy about it," suggests Chiang, "[this] was a real fantasy element. I said to Justin, 'I'm having a real problem with getting my head around this, which is a bit magical,' and we talked about it for a long time. It's Jaylah's trap, but how do we do it without it being a resin wall? And that's why it ended up being this frozen resin. Freezing smoke.

"We knew, narratively, what it needed to do in the quarry scene, the motorbike sequence," Chiang continues, "And we needed to set up these barriers so that Kirk could cause chaos and protect the *Enterprise* crew while they escape,

Jaylah's security system was a "fantasy element"

so we developed this idea that it would freeze, smoke would freeze, because that was Jaylah's trap, but then how do we transcend that into the quarry? It took ages! I mean, 20 versions."

"WHEN SHOTS WANDER TOO FAR AWAY FROM BEING GROUNDED BY A BIT OF REALITY IN THE FOREGROUND, THAT'S WHEN THEY START TO LOOK HOKEY."

reference material was an adventure in itself.

"To get there we took a commercial flight to Whitehorse (the Yukon's largest conurbation, with a population of just 12,000), and then we had to take a bi-plane, land on a lake, and from there it was a helicopter ride into the Cirque of the Unclimbables," he continues, "I mean, we're way out in the wilderness here, and there's these fantastic geological structures in this otherwise traditional Canadian landscape. As you approach it, you kind of think, 'what is that?'

"Justin always wanted Altamid to be a planet in turmoil," explains Chiang, "that Krall was really raping it, like he's sucking the life out of it, so the mining

aspect was very much part of the idea of just eating away at the planet. I took inspiration from when a nuclear submarine breaks out in the polar ice caps, there's that kind of turmoil, and if you look at the rock structures they're very much as if something has disturbed it, the tectonic plates have moved or something.

"Justin drew a petaled flower, like a rose, and that became the basis of Krall's lair. The rocks became this kind of petal idea, and linking the petals is this finger print of ravines and gullies (which Kirk rides his motorbike through). Its unsettling, jagged, a bit 'something's not quite right here.' That was the kind of subconscious idea that we wanted to sell."

TREK TRIVIA: SWARMSHIPS

Krall's swarmships have several stages of swarming behavior, from a "random mode," which is very organic and insect-like, through to "attack mode," which is mathematical and precise.

Flying at between 250mph and 500mph scale speed when swarming around the *Enterprise*, there are up to 48,000 swarmships in some shots during the *Enterprise* takedown sequence. There are approximately 6,000,000 in the wave formation during the space battle at the end of the movie.

DOUBLE ENTERPRISE

Altamid would be the final resting place for the *Enterprise*, which had already narrowly escaped destruction in the previous two movies. While the construction of the *NCC-1701-A* would make for an impressive finale, the *Enterprise* we see in the first shots of the movie had already undergone some subtle design reworking, all in service of the movie's narrative.

"Because the story is very much about vulnerability and separation – the crew gets separated, the ship should get separated – you need that fine weakness within the design," reasons Chiang on the tweaks made to the ship, "Justin wanted to go back [to the original], so we made the nacelle arms thinner, we made the neck slightly thinner and longer. It was harkening back to the 1966 version of the ship."

Having researched the original series extensively, Chiang is full of praise for its iconic shots of the *Enterprise* in flight, saying "They found the ultimate way of displaying the *Enterprise*. Some of [our] shots refer back to that, just because there's no other way of doing it!"

Despite this, his team were keen to explore "that beautiful shape" in new ways. "We really wanted to introduce new things, and Justin was very much into that," Chiang continues, "wanting to show the audiences new parts of the ship, new angles that you hadn't seen before."

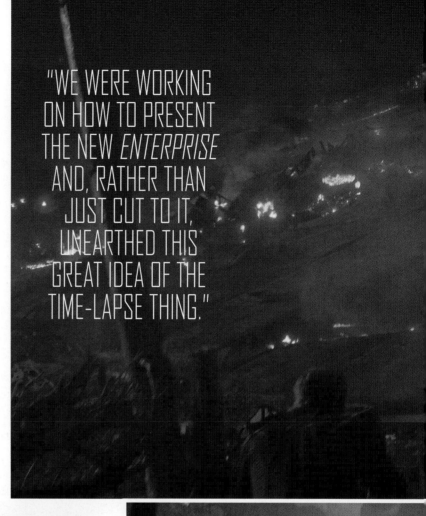

"WE WERE WORKING ON HOW TO PRESENT THE NEW *ENTERPRISE* AND, RATHER THAN JUST CUT TO IT, UNEARTHED THIS GREAT IDEA OF THE TIME-LAPSE THING."

FINAL CUT

With its truncated production schedule, it's no surprise to learn that work was ongoing to complete the movie – even after it premiered in Australia on July 6th.

"Oh my god, if I told you that I flew on the 9th of July..." Chiang smiles, "I was still working on it. So, the Australian version ended up being a version that will never be seen again. I was working on the 8th, I was in Los Angeles, I flew back on the 9th, spent a day in DI (Digital Intermediate – the final digital print of the movie), still reviewing shots with Justin, and on the 10th he finished the DI. On the 12th we had the British premier, so that's how tight it was."

The last sign-off came down to three effects shots, including a refractor shot that was pulled out, and one of Krall at the start of the zero gravity sequence that Chiang still feels they never got quite right.

"I always describe it as a number of goes and, for me, a shot probably takes in the region of anywhere between five to ten goes," says Chiang, "I was probably two or three out on where I wanted to be on that. I've never delivered a film this close to the wire, in terms of what we needed. We pushed it to the very limit. I mean, we got it done, but my god, a couple of weeks out we were three hundreds shots [away]. Everybody worked incredibly hard to deliver it, but it was pretty tight."

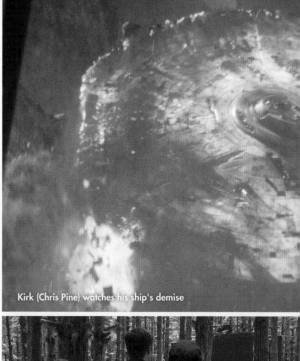

Kirk (Chris Pine) watches his ship's demise

Chris Pine and Anton Yelchin stare at a green screen...

TREK TRIVIA: U.S.S. ENTERPRISE 1701-A

In keeping with the revised fragility of its immediate predecessor, the new *Enterprise*, designed by Shaun Hogrid, looked towards Matt Jefferies' original classic design for inspiration – the engine nacelles are longer and thinner, with the pylons connecting them to the hull sweeping back but with a horizontal front edge that references the silhouette of the original more closely. The neck is further forward than the J.J. Abrams version, and angle of the edge of the main saucer section matches the original *1701*.

A full CG build (with interior framework) of the new *Enterprise* was completed by Double Negative in 3 weeks, ensuring the entire ship could be seen in extreme close-up and from every angle during the roving camera move that would make up the timelapse construction sequence. In real world terms (that is, from Kirk and his crew's perspective), the *Enterprise*-A construction took a little over a month – more than enough time for a stretch of shore leave.

Matt Jefferies iconic original *Enterprise* design

The *Enterprise* burns (*Star Trek Beyond*)

With the more vulnerable original torn to shreds by Krall's drone fleet, a new *Enterprise* was required if Kirk and crew were to boldly go on any further missions. The striking timelapse-style sequence that closes the film was devised just six weeks prior to the scheduled completion of effects work on the film.

"It was the last thing that Justin wanted," Chiang reveals of the new ship, designed by Shaun Hogrid. "We were working on how to present the new *Enterprise* and, rather than just cut to it, unearthed this great idea of the time-lapse thing. And, of course, you can imagine the kind of work in building the geometry. I have to say, under Raymond Chen (supervisor on the project at Double Negative's Canadian facility), his team did a fantastic job of building it, because they had to work out where all the corridors are from the blueprints of the original *Enterprise*. The team did a fantastic job in just a short space of time to get that shot together."

The sequence also gave Chiang and visual effects producer Ron Aimes an opportunity to don space suits and make multiple cameos in the movie. "We shot green-screen sprites of people building it," Chiang laughs, "so when you sweep around the top of the dish, all those little people are Ron and myself, building." ⟶

...which is replaced by the downed *Enterprise* in the final shot

THE WORLD PREMIERE

In a specially erected outdoor arena, San Diego Comic-Con 2016 played host to the official World Premiere of *Star Trek Beyond*.

Words: Ian Spelling

Paramount Pictures launched *Star Trek Beyond* with a star-studded, blockbuster premiere event on the opening day of San Diego Comic-Con, July 22nd, 2016. The studio took over Marina Park for the festivities, welcoming thousands of Comic-Con attendees lucky enough to secure themselves a free ticket to an outdoor IMAX screening – the first-ever such event for an IMAX projection.

As fans queued up to enter, the cast and crew were busy meeting the press for a bustling red carpet session. Attending the screening were stars Chris Pine, Zachary Quinto, Zoe Saldana, Simon Pegg, Karl Urban, John Cho, Idris Elba, Sofia Boutella, Shohreh Aghdashloo, and Deep Roy, along with director Justin Lin, producer J.J. Abrams, composer Michael Giacchino, and many others.

GETTING COMFORTABLE

Meanwhile, inside the main arena, fans were treated to a screening of the original 1960s *Star Trek* episode, "The Corbomite Maneuver," and Rihanna's music video for her *Beyond* theme song, "Sledgehammer." The place went crazy when Nichelle Nichols, *Star Trek*'s original Uhura, graced the stage and spoke to the *Trek* faithful, clearly enjoying the love that flooded back from her audience.

A costume contest added to the fun, as did giveaways of free food, and a very welcome commemorative seat cushion, which made for a much more comfortable viewing experience! In fact, all attendees left with a swagbag of mementos from

Fans prepare to go Beyond...

The stars of *Star Trek Beyond* gather on the San Diego red carpet with director Justin Lin and J.J.Abrams (Left to right: Chris Pine, John Cho, Karl Urban, Simon Pegg, Zachary Quinto, Lin, Zoe Saldana, Sofia Boutella, and Abrams)

the event, including a Vulcan baseball cap, a premiere T-shirt, and a selection of *Trek* blu-rays.

Then it was time for the screening, or almost time. First, as the sun set, comedian Conan O'Brien warmed up the crowd with some *Trek*-flavored jokes. He then introduced the cast, Lin, and Abrams. At this point it was dark, and the San Diego Symphony Orchestra kicked in with a live performance of *Star Trek* music, accompanied by a dazzling display of fireworks, lasers, and smoke.

Prior to the film, Zachary Quinto paid tribute to his friend and mentor, Leonard Nimoy, while Abrams mourned the loss of Anton Yelchin. The actors and filmmakers wore black delta-shield pins, made especially for the occasion to honor Yelchin, and the producer also revealed that Yelchin's parents – Irina and Viktor – were in the audience. "He should be here tonight," Abrams noted, requesting a moment of silence. The actors joined Abrams and Lin in a group hug before exiting the stage.

Finally, this epic and emotional event reached its climax, with the official world premiere of *Star Trek Beyond*, to the accompaniment of the San Diego Symphony Orchestra, who performed the movie's entire score live.

Fans line up for the cosplay competition

The audience enjoy the event

Justin Lin, J.J. Abrams and Zoe Saldana

Simon Pegg signs autographs

While the San Diego Comic-con event was the official world premiere for *Star Trek Beyond*, the movie had already been screened at premieres in Sydney, Australia, and in London, UK.

With castmembers in attendance on both red carpets (although the London one was white), co-writer and Scotty star Simon Pegg introduced the movie at each premiere with an emotional tribute to the late Anton Yelchin.

Shoreh Aghdashloo and Idris Elba

STAR TREK™
BEYOND
REVIEWED

By Christopher Cooper

Spock (Zachary Quinto) and Bones (Karl Urban)

My Mom and I emerged from the local multiplex, breathless and blinking, into the bright July sunshine. "That was proper, old-fashioned *Star Trek*!" she enthused, clearly delighted, if a little frazzled by the breakneck pace of Justin Lin's *Star Trek Beyond*. I'm pretty sure I saw her punch the air as she said it, which isn't like her at all.

Judging by the response of the rest of the audience that was streaming out of the cinema around us, and the smile on my own face, we all felt the same way. We'd enjoyed the shared experience of watching

BEATS AND SHOUTING

It's long been held that odd-numbered *Star Trek* films aren't necessarily the finest exemplars of the franchise. As the 13th *Trek* movie overall, and the third in the *Kelvin Timeline* sequence, did *Star Trek Beyond* finally kick that urban myth firmly into touch?

Kirk (Chris Pine) hatches a desperate plan to save his crew

a good, fun *Star Trek* movie together, with plenty to keep both regular movie-goers and we *Trek* old-timers happy – but that's not how I felt after seeing it for the first time. Let me explain.

Abusing my position as editor of this magazine, I'd scored a seat at the London premiere of *Beyond* a few weeks earlier. It was a typical, British summer's day – heavy rain interrupted by occasional bursts of sunlight. On the white (and very damp) "red" carpet, the only star I'd glimpsed was the back of Idris Elba's head, as he'd signed

autographs for some very patient fans. As the assembled press didn't seem to want to speak to me (I know! Don't they know who I am?), I made my way inside Leicester Square's Empire cinema, found my seat up in the gods, and settled down in anticipation. Or was it nervousness?

The audience, whoever they were, had their glad-rags on. Smart suits, short skirts, a dizzying array of perfumes – this was an event; this was special; excitement filled the air – but were these people more excited about seeing the

latest *Star Trek,* or by the glamor of attending a movie premiere?

Was I excited? All I could feel was the weight of my reviewer's hat, pressing heavily upon my shoulders. If there's one thing that's bound to distance you from a movie, it's knowing you have to write about it. I worried that I wouldn't enjoy it, that I'd spend the next two hours with a critical demon whispering bad thoughts in my ear, akin to Krall's bitter recriminations against the Federation.

I felt… alone.

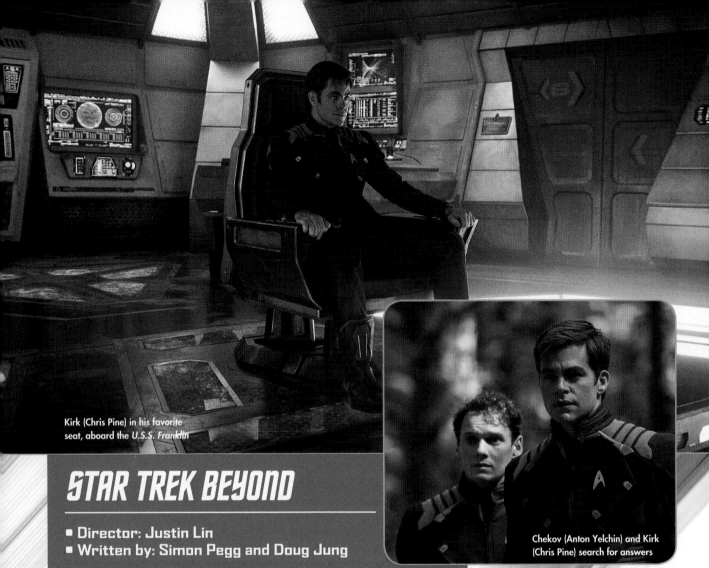

Kirk (Chris Pine) in his favorite seat, aboard the U.S.S. Franklin

Chekov (Anton Yelchin) and Kirk (Chris Pine) search for answers

STAR TREK BEYOND

- **Director: Justin Lin**
- **Written by: Simon Pegg and Doug Jung**

On the Federation's newest starbase, *U.S.S. Yorktown*, shore leave is cut short for the *Enterprise* crew when an escape pod is recovered near an impenetrable nebula. The pod's occupant, an alien named Kalara, begs for help to recover her crew, stranded deep inside the nebula on the planet Altamid.

However, no sooner has the *Enterpise* crossed through the nebula than it is ambushed by a swarm of alien ships. Krall, the commander of the swarm, is hunting for an ancient weapon he knows to be carried aboard the *Enterprise*, but Kirk has hidden it. As the ship is torn apart by the swarm, the crew abandon ship – only to be captured by Krall's forces. The saucer section crashes onto the planet below.

Kirk, Chekov, and Kalara return to the downed *Enterprise*, where it is revealed that Kalara was working for Krall all along – the whole mission was a trap. Kalara is killed as Kirk and Chekov escape.

Bones and Spock have made it safely to the planet, but Spock is wounded and in urgent need of medical aid. Meanwhile,

Scotty meets Jaylah, an outsider who has been trapped on Altamid for some years.

Sulu and Uhura escape from Krall's cells, but are recaptured after discovering that the alien has been monitoring Starfleet communications, and intends to attack *Yorktown* – and then the Federation – with the alien weapon he has recovered from one of the *Enterprise* crew.

Kirk and Chekov are reunited with Scotty, and Jaylah shows them her "house," where she has been hiding out – it's the *U.S.S. Franklin*, a Federation ship that mysteriously went missing a century before. Scotty beams Spock and Bones to safety, and they hatch a plan to rescue the remaining crew from Krall's base.

When Krall departs with his drone fleet to attack *Yorktown*, the *Enterprise* crew take off in pursuit aboard the repaired *Franklin*. The deadly chase to stop Krall ends with a devastating discovery – Krall was once Balthazar Edison, the *Franklin*'s captain and a former soldier who fought against the Xindi and the Romulans. Edison has extended his life using alien technology, transforming into Krall while plotting revenge against the Federation that he believes abandoned him.

Beyond pressed all the right buttons for me during that first viewing, don't get me wrong, but seeing the movie again – crucially with my Mom and a bunch of other *Star Trek* fans, old and new, who'd packed out a local cinema on the movie's opening weekend – I appreciated it so much more. My enjoyment fed off the response of those around me, and perhaps that's a reflection of the underlying message of *Beyond*, and the big "*Star Trek*" idea at its heart – that in unity there is strength.

BEYOND *INSURRECTION*

While *Star Trek: Insurrection* made a movie out of what could have easily been a *Next Generation* TV script (with a TV budget to match), *Star Trek Beyond* looks every bit the modern effects-laden blockbuster, while being arguably the closest a *Trek* movie has ever come to accurately adapting the original 1960s source material for the big screen.

J.J. Abrams' 2009 movie captured the gung-ho spirit of the original, aided in no small part by the perfectly cast young actors filling its iconic roles, but it was clearly more popcorn movie than a Roddenberry-esque musing on the human condition. Later, *Into Darkness* came fully-loaded

Scotty (Simon Pegg) and Jaylah (Sophia Boutella) struggle to protect *Yorktown* from Krall's evil plan

Uhura (Zoe Saldana) and Sulu (John Cho) captured by Krall

AS MANY REVIEWERS AND FANS QUICKLY POINTED OUT, *BEYOND* GENUINELY FEELS LIKE AN EPISODE FROM THE ORIGINAL SERIES.

with allegory and "Big Ideas," but earned itself a critical backlash thanks to its self-referential riffing on previous *Star Trek* storylines. As many reviewers and fans quickly pointed out, *Beyond* genuinely feels like an episode from the original series, albeit layered with whizz-bang effects and the frenetic cinematography familiar to fans of Justin Lin's turbo-charged pictures. It's a combination of storytelling techniques that, perhaps surprisingly, works extremely well, and proves you should never pre-judge a finished movie on the basis of a teaser trailer...

Structurally, *Beyond* hits all the beats required of the TV incarnation: a central mystery for the crew to unravel, drop-kicking Kirk fight scenes, Spock and McCoy's razor-sharp retorts, and a shock reveal that puts events into perspective. And it's funny too. Really funny.

Simon Pegg and Doug Jung's appreciation and understanding of what makes *Star Trek* tick is more than evident, as is their diligence in crafting a script that is straightforward, finely-tuned, and way more watertight than a Tribble with magic blood.

This is particularly impressive given the relatively short development time the writers had

to pull their story together, and indicative of the attention they paid on-set during production, refining scenes until each carries its own weight and moves the picture forward. While it's fair to say that *Beyond* lacks narrative complexity, first and foremost this is a character piece. Krall's villainy poses the required deadly threat to the galaxy, and his motives and reasoning are slowly revealed to be selfishly human, and while we ultimately recognize that he's stone-cold bonkers, we can understand how he got there. If his rage is what an extended stay in deep space can do to a man, no wonder Kirk is thinking about his career options! Krall's journey isn't that far removed from Kirk's, but our opinion of and confidence in Kirk is only increased by how our hero reacts to the similar situation he and his crew find themselves in.

Equally, *Beyond* is confident enough in its themes that it sets them up and then leaves its audience to follow them through, without feeling the need to add clunky expository dialogue (not counting occasional spurts of technobabble, but hey, this is *Star Trek*!)

In an early scene, extraordinarily reminiscent of Captain Pike's famously melancholic exchange with Dr. Boyce in the first *Star Trek* pilot episode, "The Cage," we find Kirk in reflective mood, questioning his future in Starfleet. His arc is set up in a few lines, but it's through Chris Pine's most accomplished performance yet as Kirk that we follow that story to its inevitable conclusion. As Bones (Karl Urban) tells Spock in another scene, "There's no need to say it."

ABSENT FRIENDS

Given that there are subtle (and some less so) nods to *Trek*'s 50th anniversary throughout, *Beyond* deftly fulfils Paramount Pictures' edict that this third movie be less "*Star Trekky*," by not allowing itself to get bogged down in the continuity issues that provided both the narrative spark for *Star Trek (2009)*, and problems for *Into Darkness*. Ironically, this effectively makes it more "*Star Trekky*" than any previous movie (including those starring the original cast), allowing it to be more "episodic" and self-contained, with just a light dusting of in-universe continuity to give depth and color to Kirk and Spock's character development. It's a refreshing step in the right direction for the *Kelvin* Timeline.

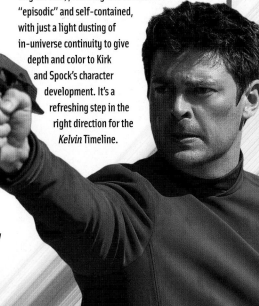

Idris Elba's menacing Krall

Justin Lin and Chris Pine on
the set of *Star Trek Beyond*

AMID ALL THE ENTERTAINING "BEATS AND SHOUTING" OF LIN'S FLUID STYLE, *BEYOND*'S TRUE STRENGTH LIES ENTIRELY IN ITS CHARACTERS.

That said, one moment of pure continuity can't have left a dry eye in the house, as Spock (Zachary Quinto, again excellent in the role) opens a Vulcan picture frame left to him in Spock Prime's personal effects, to reveal a photograph of the *original* original crew, circa *The Final Frontier*. It's a thoughtful and respectful homage to that group of actors, *Star Trek*'s anniversary, and to the late Leonard Nimoy.

Another bittersweet but rather beautiful moment, near the end of the film, is also worthy of note, and I feel certain it was a late edit following the tragic death of Anton Yelchin (Chekov). Following the crew's travails at the hands of Krall, during which many lives were lost, Kirk raises a glass to "Absent Friends." The shot cuts to the group of crew members to whom Kirk is speaking, which includes the young Ensign. The movie is dedicated to both Yelchin and Nimoy, and *Star Trek* is poorer for the loss of both fine actors.

VICE-ADMIRALS DON'T FLY

Amid all the entertaining "beats and shouting" of Lin's fluid style, *Beyond*'s true strength lies entirely in its characters. Idris Elba as Krall is a menacing presence, and Elba externalizes his character's inner pain with a powerful physicality. But it's poster-girl Jaylah (Sofia Boutella) who absolutely steals the movie. In two scenes in particular, one without a word of dialogue, Boutella conveys all the hurt and trauma her character has endured with understated subtlety. Jaylah also has a similar taste in music to

one J.J. Abrams, providing one of the high points of the movie.

Set three years into the five-year mission, *Beyond* also finally gives the returning ensemble the chance to play their characters as the mature unit we met back in 1966 – and they clearly relish it. Their camaraderie leaps off the screen and, after three movies, we have a closer relationship with these actors in these parts too, in a way we haven't before. We're as comfortable with Pine, Urban, Quinto, Yelchin, Zoe Saldana (Uhura), John Cho (Sulu), and Simon Pegg (Scotty) in their roles as we are with William Shatner, DeForest Kelley, Leonard Nimoy, Walter Koenig, Nichelle Nichols, George Takei, and James Doohan.

In paying tribute to *Star Trek*'s 50th anniversary, Lin, Pegg, Jung, and their cast and crew have taken the franchise full circle, and proven that there will always be new frontiers to explore in Gene Roddenberry's universe. Here's to the next adventure of the starship *Enterprise* (just how *will* George Kirk fit in...?) ⋀